3 English Language Arts

New York

New York
Ready
Instruction

Curriculum Associates

Illustration Credits:
Kathie Kelleher: pages 11, 44
Ruth Flanagan: page 36

Photography Credits:
page 27 © Carl Van Vechten/wikimedia.com
page 52 © Yanzomme/Dreamstime.com
page 86 © clipart.com

Project Manager: Nicole Jackson
Cover Design: Matthew Pollock
Book Design: Pat Lucas and Kelli Rossetti

ISBN 978-0-7609-6456-9
©2010—Curriculum Associates, LLC
North Billerica, MA 01862

Table of Contents

To the Student

All students need good reading and writing skills to be successful. **New York—Ready English Language Arts Instruction** will help you develop the ELA skills every third grader should know. New York calls these skills Core Performance Indicators (CPIs) and Grade-Specific Performance Indicators (GPIs). Each lesson in this book teaches CPIs and GPIs. Learning the CPIs and GPIs in this book will make you a stronger reader and writer. It will also help you do well on the grade 3 New York Testing Program English Language Arts Test.

Your teacher will tell you what lessons you will work on in this book. Each lesson has five parts. Your teacher will guide you through some parts of the lesson. You will work on the other parts on your own. You will read passages and answer questions. **Think About It** questions may help you answer these questions. **Hints** may also help you answer the questions. Most lessons end with a two-page passage. It is followed by four to six multiple-choice and short-response questions. You will also practice answering questions about a listening selection and correcting errors in editing paragraphs. The passages and questions are just like the types you will see on the New York Testing Program English Language Arts Test.

Tips for Answering Multiple-Choice and Short-Response Questions

- Read each problem carefully before you try to answer it.

- Be sure you know what the question is asking you to do.

- For multiple-choice questions, read all the answer choices before you choose your answer. Then cross out any answer choices that you know are wrong. Think about the answer choices that are left. Choose the one you think is correct. Then, circle the letter of the correct answer choice or fill in the answer bubble on the answer form.

- For short-response questions, be sure you answer the question you are being asked. Also, support your answer using details from the passage. Write your answer on the lines or space provided.

- Read the question one more time. Then check that your answer makes sense.

GPI/CPI

3.R.CPI.2: Use context to determine meaning

3.R.CPI.11: Determine the meaning of unfamiliar words

Introduction

In this lesson, you will learn how to find out what words mean. For example, what is an orange? Is it a color? Or is it a fruit? You can't know which meaning is right without reading the word in a sentence. That's because the word *orange* has more than one meaning.

Some words have many meanings. Others are just new to you. When you read the sentences and paragraphs around a word, you are looking at that word's **context**. When you use context, you see how a word is used.

Sometimes, though, authors use words in new ways. For example, think about the sentence "The cold wind bites at my nose." Now think about what *bites* means. Can wind bite? No. But by using the word *bite*, the author shows us that the wind is so cold that it hurts.

Finally, you can break a word into parts to find its meaning. For example, think of the word *colorful.* If you break the word into parts, you get this:

color + ful = colorful

Based on this, you can see that *colorful* means "full of color."

Here's a chart that shows how you might find out what a word means.

What Does This Word Mean?

Word	Word in a Sentence	What I Think the Word Means	Words That Helped Me
daffodil	The pretty daffodil bloomed in the field.	a type of flower	"pretty," "bloomed," "field"

Read this poem. Then answer the question below.

Old Blue

When I was a girl, my grandpa
Took me for a ride on his tractor.
He called it Old Blue, the color of sky.
"This thing is <u>ancient</u>!" he'd say with a <u>grin</u>,
5   And talk about days long ago.
"After so many years working on this farm,
It's been a while since Old Blue was new!"

In the poem, what does the word *ancient* mean?

▶ First, find the word *ancient* in the poem. It is in the fourth line.

▶ What does the word *ancient* tell about? It tells about Grandpa's tractor.

▶ Now look at the context. What else do you know about the tractor? It is called Old Blue. Grandpa has used it on the farm for many years.

▶ Add up the clues to make a guess. Old Blue must be old. That means the word *ancient* must mean "very old."

ANSWER: In the poem, the word *ancient* means "very old."

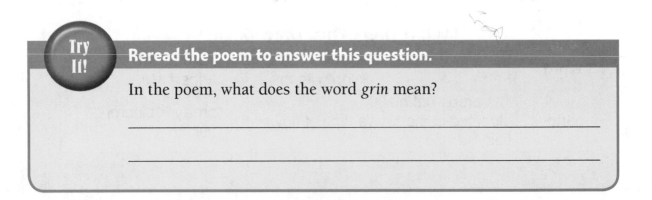

Try It! **Reread the poem to answer this question.**

In the poem, what does the word *grin* mean?

_____

_____

Read the postcard. Use the Think About It to guide your reading. Then answer the question. Use the Hint to help you.

Think About It

Which words best tell about Jonathan in the passage?

Hint

Read the words around the sentence that has the word *patience* in it.

Postcard from Camp

Hello, Mom and Dad!

    I am having a wonderful time at camp! We learned how to play water polo. It took a long time to learn, but I stayed calm. My <u>patience</u> paid off when my team won first place. That reminded me how much I really love learning new sports!

Love, Jonathan

Which words from the postcard above tell what *patience* means?

A   "wonderful time"

B   "stayed calm"

C   "won first place"

D   "learning new sports"

CORRECT ANSWER   The second answer choice is correct.

SUPPORTING DETAILS   The words "stayed calm" give you a big clue. These words help the reader know that Jonathan does not get mad or give up.

INCORRECT ANSWERS   The first answer choice is not correct because it doesn't tell about how Jonathan acts when playing water polo.

The third answer choice is not correct because the word *patience* tells what Jonathan needs to learn the game, not to win it.

The fourth answer choice is not correct because playing and winning help Jonathan remember why he loves learning new sports.

Read the story. Use each Think About It to guide your reading.

Tiger Splash Park

Think About It

Why does the family look at a map when they get to the park?

Gabe wants to see animal shows. How would he probably act while watching the shows?

Think about what this paragraph tells about. What do the family members do before they have lunch?

1   If your family wants to get away, head to Tiger Splash Park. It's a fun place for both kids and grown-ups. And the entrance fee is only $10 for adults and $6 for teens. Kids under 12 get in free.

2   Last weekend, my family and I got to the water park early. We were all curious to know about what the park offers, so we looked at a map. We had a lot of choices! There were animal shows and roller coasters and water rides.

3   My daughter, Angel, is brave. She wanted to check out the fast rides. My son, Gabe, is a quiet animal lover. He wanted to settle into a seat and watch all of the shows.

4   My husband, Eddie, also loves animals. The two of them went to see the Big Cat Show. But I am as fearless as Angel. She and I headed to one of the park's roller coasters.

5   The lines were not long, and Angel and I rode all six roller coasters, one after another. The first one scared Angel a bit. She looked over at me with big eyes and said, "Do you really think this ride is safe?" Once the ride began, though, she laughed and shouted happily at all the twists and turns.

6   Finally, we reunited with Gabe and Eddie. As we sat down to eat lunch, they said the Big Cat Show was the best thing about the park. Angel and I thought that the Brain Mixer was better than anything. Next time, we will trade plans and see who is right!

Use the Hints to answer the questions below. Circle the letter for each correct answer. Provide supporting details.

Look at paragraph 2. The family looks at a map of the park. Why do they do this?

1   At the beginning of the story, the family is curious. The word *curious* means

   A   got lost right away.

   (B) wanted to learn more.

   C   couldn't make a choice.

   D   got somewhere early.

Supporting Details: B is right because the family wanted to know what park offers

Reread paragraph 3. How would someone who wants to see the shows most likely act?

2   What does Gabe do when he settles into a seat and watches animal shows?

   (A) stays still and doesn't leave

   B   moves around in his seat a lot

   C   gets bored and goes on a ride

   D   tries to get close to the animals

Supporting Details: Gabe was quiet, so he would behave

Look at paragraph 6. What context clues can help you understand the meaning of reunited?

3   Read this sentence from the story.

   "Finally, we reunited with Gabe and Eddie."

The word *reunited* most likely means Angel and her mother

   A   went on more roller coasters.

   B   agreed to go to the park again.

   (C) joined their family members.

   D   looked at the map again.

Supporting Details: At the end they were with Gabe and Eddie

PAIR SHARE

With your partner, share and discuss your answers and supporting details.

Directions
Read this passage. Then answer questions 1 through 5.

A Second-Hand Time Machine

by Bryce Bixler

My grandma rocks! She dresses in her own way, with big jewelry and bright colors. She has white braids that stick out from under her crazy hats. And she laughs really loudly. When we go out together, people always smile and give us little waves.

A few weeks ago, we went to the park to fly Gram's kite. Gram saw a guy selling balloons. She got a dreamy look in her eyes and remembered a story. She said that when she was a little girl, she loved balloons. One day, her dad bought all of the balloons in Central Park. That must have been a lot. Gram floated over the park for hours! Eventually, people threw darts at the balloons so they would pop, and Gram came down.

When I told my dad about the balloon story, he shook his head and laughed. He said, "That woman has always been full of beans." I guess he thinks Gram makes stuff up, but I always believe her. It's just more fun that way.

Of course, when Gram asked if I wanted to go to the second-hand clothing store last weekend, I said yes. She picked me up early, and we stopped for donuts on the way.

When we got to the store, Gram's eyes lit up. "So many bargains!" she exclaimed. "A little bit of money can buy a lot in this store!"

As soon as we walked in the door, we went directly to the hats. Gram put on a black one with a veil that covered her face. Then she acted all sad, pretending that her fish had just died and she was burying him. When she put that hat down, she picked up a man's hat with a deep crease down the middle. She called it a fedora. When she put it on my head, she said, "Look at you. You're such a handsome boy! Let's get you a jacket and tie."

Before I knew what was happening, I was dressed like an old-time movie star. Gram kept calling me Bogart and said that she needed some new clothes so that we would look right together. She went into a small room to try on some clothes.

"Look at this fancy thing! Isn't this elegant?" Gram said as she returned. She was wearing an old-fashioned dress with lace and a bow at the waist. She had her braids all pinned up on her head. She looked like a movie star, too. It was such a big change, she almost didn't look like Gram anymore.

I told Gram that she looked beautiful. She smiled. "We should take some pictures to remember this moment forever," she said. So she took out her cell phone and did just that. We had fun, posing like movie stars. We even had the saleswoman take some shots of us dancing together.

"I always used to think I would be famous," Gram said while striking a pose. I told her that she is super famous to me, and she looked really happy.

We bought the clothes and headed home. On the way, Gram said that maybe she and I should take some dance lessons!

1 Read this sentence from the story.

> **Eventually, people threw darts at the balloons so they would pop, and Gram came down.**

In this sentence, the word "eventually" **most likely** means

A before an event
B after a time
C with great feeling
D instead of another thing

2 The story says that Gram's "eyes lit up." This phrase **most likely** means that Gram is

A excited
B bored
C sleepy
D joking

3 In the story, Grandma says that the store has many bargains. What does the word "bargain" mean?

A fancy clothes and shoes
B bright colors
C a thing that costs little money
D strange sights

4 The story says that Gram and her grandson go directly to the hats. What does the word "directly" mean?

A with care
B slowly
C happily
D right away

5 Read these sentences from the story.

> **"Look at this fancy thing! Isn't this elegant?"**

This sentence tells you that the dress

A looks nice
B looks old
C costs a lot of money
D doesn't fit Gram

Answer Form

1 Ⓐ Ⓑ Ⓒ Ⓓ
2 Ⓐ Ⓑ Ⓒ Ⓓ
3 Ⓐ Ⓑ Ⓒ Ⓓ
4 Ⓐ Ⓑ Ⓒ Ⓓ
5 Ⓐ Ⓑ Ⓒ Ⓓ

Number Correct

/ 5

GPI/CPI 3.R.CPI.2, 3.R.CPI.11   New York

GPI/CPI

3.R.GPI.1e: Identify main ideas and details in informational texts

3.R.GPI.1j: Identify conclusions

3.R.GPI.2n: Summarize main ideas and details in imaginative texts

Introduction

In this lesson, you will learn about the main idea. The **main idea** is what an article or story is mostly about.

Pretend you are talking with a friend. You say, "I just a read a story about a robot who saves the world." Guess what? You've just told your friend the story's main idea. You didn't need to tell all the little details. You didn't say that the robot was green or that it loved to eat bananas peels. One sentence was enough.

Sometimes, you can find the main idea in the title. For example, "The Robot Who Saved the World" tells the main idea. Articles have main ideas, too. Many times, this idea is in the introduction or conclusion. **Introductions** come at the beginning of articles. **Conclusions** are at the end of articles. They retell what the article is mostly about.

But remember, the main idea of a story is different from its theme. A **theme** is a story's lesson or message.

Use this chart to help you find the main idea in a passage.

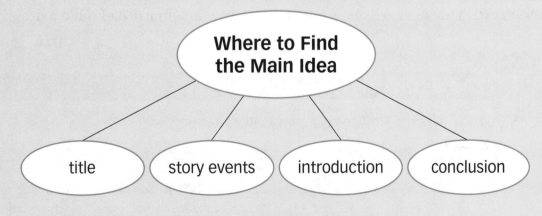

©Curriculum Associates   Copying is not permitted.

Read this story. Then answer the question below.

The Deck

1   Every Saturday, Sara helps her dad. One week, she carried a bag of groceries from the car. Another week, Dad was washing windows. Sara gladly helped. But this week was different. This week, her dad was building a deck.

2   Sara's dad used a saw to cut long boards. Sara was afraid of the electric saw. Dad also loudly drilled holes. But Sara was afraid of the electric drill. Then Sara's dad gave her a small hammer. He pounded a nail to show her how. Then Sara did it. It worked! "This is going to be the best deck!" she said proudly.

What is this story mostly about?

▶ What do most of the sentences tell about? Most of the sentences tell about Sara and her dad.

▶ What do the sentences say about Sara and her dad? They tell that Sara likes to help her dad.

▶ What does Sara's dad need help with in the story? Read the title for a clue. Sara's dad needs help building a deck.

▶ Is it important that Sara helps her dad wash windows? No, it is not.

ANSWER: This story tells how Sara finds a way to help her dad build a deck.

Try It!

Reread the story to answer this question.

What is the first paragraph mostly about?

The first Paragraph was mostly about
Sara helping her dad every week.

Read the poem. Use the Think About It to guide your reading. Then answer the question. Use the Hint to help you.

Think About It

Read the title. Then ask yourself what most of the lines tell about it.

Carlos the Owl

Nighttime is for most owls, except for one.

Carlos the Owl hated the nighttime.

Each night, the owls left their trees to find mice to eat.

Carlos loved to eat mice, too—the gray ones were best—

5   But he was too scared to look for them in the dark.

So closing his eyes, Carlos listened for mice,

And Carlos ate his fill every single night.

This poem is mostly about an owl who hates

A flying.

B eating mice.

C the dark.

D other owls.

Hint

What is the owl's problem? What does he do to find mice?

CORRECT ANSWER   The third answer choice is correct.

SUPPORTING DETAILS   Carlos hates the dark. He is scared of it, so he closes his eyes. He listens for the mice instead of looking for them.

INCORRECT ANSWERS   The first answer choice is not correct because the poem does not say anything about Carlos flying.

The second answer choice is not correct because Carlos loves mice. He eats his fill "every single night."

The fourth answer choice is not correct because the poem does not tell how Carlos feels about other owls.

Think About It

Read the title first. It helps you learn about the important ideas in a passage.

Who is the article about? What are you learning about this person?

What happened in America while Walt was alive?

Read the article. Use each Think About It to guide your reading.

Walt Whitman: Poet of America

1   Walt Whitman is an important person in American history. He was born in New York in 1819. He had six brothers. Three of them were named for American presidents. (Those presidents were Andrew Jackson, George Washington, and Thomas Jefferson.) But it was young Walt, not his brothers, who became an important American.

2   Walt was not a president. He was a poet. In 1855, he wrote a book of poems called *Leaves of Grass*. The poems were not like most other poems at the time. They were long, and they didn't always rhyme.

3   *Leaves of Grass* was about the many different places in America, from the mountains to the plains. It was about the many different people in America, too, from the farmers to the shopkeepers. It was about being yourself. *Leaves of Grass* was about being American.

4   Walt lived during a hard time for America. During the Civil War, the North fought the South. Walt worked as a nurse, but he also kept writing. He wrote a poem to honor President Abraham Lincoln. He added this and other poems to *Leaves of Grass*.

5   Walt died in 1892. By then, the Civil War was over. America was one country again. And the most American of its poets was the New Yorker Walt Whitman.

Hints

Look at each paragraph. What are most of the paragraphs about?

Which title tells the most about what the whole article is about?

Which sentence tells you the most about the article's main idea?

PAIR SHARE

With your partner, share and discuss your answers and supporting details.

Use the Hints to answer the questions below. Circle the letter for each correct answer. Provide supporting details.

1   What is this passage mostly about?

A   being a nurse during the Civil War

B   a book of poems called *Leaves of Grass*

C   brothers who were named after presidents

D   a man who wrote about America

Supporting Details: Walt wrote about America and being your self.

2   What is another good title for this passage?

A   "The Most American of Poets"

B   "A Nurse and a Writer"

C   "From Farmers to Shopkeepers"

D   "One Country Again"

Supporting Details: The title is Poet of America your saying it backwards but with most.

3   Which sentence from the passage gives the most important information?

A   "The poems were not like most other poems at the time."

B   "*Leaves of Grass* was about being American."

C   "Walt lived during a hard time for America."

D   "During the Civil War, the North fought the South."

Supporting Details: That means his poems are unige.

Directions
Read this story. Then answer questions 1 through 5.

Liberty Island, Finally!

by Brendan Wolfe

We McGinns are always running late. My brother, Kevin, is late getting up in the morning. Mom is late getting out the door to work. And I am late brushing my teeth at night. So it's no surprise that we were all late on Saturday morning, the day of our family trip to Liberty Island.

I think Dad was even more excited than me about our trip.

"Liberty Island is the home of the Statue of Liberty," he said.

"I know, Dad."

"Yes," he said, "but did you know that the statue was a gift?"

"I know that, too, Dad. It was a gift from France on America's hundredth birthday."

"You're pretty smart, Megan McGinn."

"Dad!" I said. "You have to get ready. We're running late again!"

Dad yawned and put on his shoes.

In the kitchen, Mom stood at the counter drinking her coffee. She said she could never go anywhere without first drinking her coffee. I hate the taste of coffee. I also hate how long it takes to make. Slowly, it drips into the coffee pot. *Drip, drip.* Just the sound makes me feel like I'm running late!

Mom took a sip of her coffee. "Megan, did you know that Lady Liberty holds a tablet in her left hand?" she said.

"I know, Mom."

"Yes," she said, "but do you know what is written on the tablet?"

"I know that, too, Mom. America's birthday is written on the tablet: July 4, 1776."

"You're pretty smart, Megan McGinn."

"Mom!" I said. "You have to get ready. We're running late again!"

Mom took another sip of her coffee and said that she needed to find her purse. "I can never find my purse," she said.

I looked everywhere for Kevin. Then I saw that he was under his covers. He wasn't even out of bed yet!

I yelled at my little brother, and he jumped out of the bed. He put on his favorite T-shirt, the one with the aliens on it. As he got ready, I said to him, "Kevin, do you know how big the Statue of Liberty is?"

"I don't care," he said.

"Just one of Lady Liberty's fingers is eight feet long," I said.

"That can't be right," he said. "Nothing is that big."

Then we heard Mom and Dad calling from the kitchen. It was finally time to get in the car and go.

"Finally!" I said.

But when I got to the kitchen, Mom looked at me and frowned. She asked me if I had eaten breakfast yet. I hadn't. She asked me if I had brushed my teeth. I hadn't. She asked me if I had brushed my hair. I hadn't done that, either.

"Megan McGinn!" she said. "You have to get ready. We're running late again!"

1 What is this story **mostly** about?

- **A** how a girl hates the taste of her mom's coffee
- **B** how the Statue of Liberty was a birthday gift
- **C** how a family is late for a trip to Liberty Island
- **D** how Kevin sleeps late on the day of the family trip

2 Which sentence is **most** important to the main idea of the story?

- **A** "We McGinns are always running late."
- **B** "I yelled at my little brother, and he jumped out of the bed."
- **C** "'Just one of Lady Liberty's fingers is eight feet long,' I said."
- **D** "Then we heard Mom and Dad calling from the kitchen."

3 What title would be another good title for this story?

- **A** "In a Hurry Yet Again!"
- **B** "A Statue for America's Birthday"
- **C** "The Tallest Lady in the World"
- **D** "A Brother Who Believes Nothing"

4 What are the last two paragraphs **mostly** about?

- **A** how fun the family trip is
- **B** how old the Statue of Liberty is
- **C** how the Statue of Liberty was a gift
- **D** how Megan still needs to get ready

5 This story is **mostly** about someone who is

- **A** sleeping
- **B** rushing
- **C** running
- **D** playing

Answer Form

1	Ⓐ	Ⓑ	Ⓒ	Ⓓ
2	Ⓐ	Ⓑ	Ⓒ	Ⓓ
3	Ⓐ	Ⓑ	Ⓒ	Ⓓ
4	Ⓐ	Ⓑ	Ⓒ	Ⓓ
5	Ⓐ	Ⓑ	Ⓒ	Ⓓ

Number Correct ___ / 5

Lesson 3
Supporting Details

GPI/CPI

3.R.GPI.1e: Identify main ideas and supporting details in informational texts

3.R.GPI.3a: Identify important and unimportant details

Introduction

In this lesson you will learn about details. **Supporting details** tell more about a passage's main idea. All passages have a main idea and details.

Some details in stories tell you what happens. For example, a boy takes his kite to the park. That is a detail. Other details tell you what things look like, where things happen, and who does what.

Many details in articles are facts. **Facts** are bits of information. New York is called the Empire State. That's a fact.

Some details are more important than others. They do a better job of telling about the main idea. For example, here is a main idea: Judy visits her grandmother one weekend. Some details are important. What Judy and her grandmother talk about is important. Other details are less important. What Judy eats for breakfast the day she visits is not an important detail.

Look at these charts to help you think about details in fiction and nonfiction. The chart on the left shows supporting details for an article. The chart on the right shows supporting details for a story.

Sharks are dangerous. (nonfiction main idea)

Supporting Details
They are hunters.
They can swim very fast.
They are hard to see in water.

Lisa wins a contest. (fiction main idea)

Supporting Details
She makes a painting.
She enters it into a contest.
The judge says that she is the winner.

Read this article. Then answer the question below.

Milk: Here's to a Healthy Drink

1   Many people drink milk because it is healthy. Yes, milk comes from cows, an animal found on many farms. But milk can also come from goats, camels, and horses. Milk can even come from soybeans. Still, most of the milk we drink in the United States comes from cows.

2   Milk can be used to make cheese and yogurt. These are tasty foods. But milk is not just popular because it tastes good. Milk is healthy. It keeps our bones strong and our teeth in working order.

According to the article, what is the most important thing to learn about milk?

▶   What is the article mostly about? You can find the answer in the title and in the first sentence. Milk is a healthy drink.

▶   What are the most important details? What tells you the most about milk overall?

▶   Is it important that cows are found on many farms? No, it isn't. Is it important that goats and camels give milk? No, it isn't.

ANSWER: The most important thing to learn about milk is that many people drink it because it keeps our bones strong and our teeth in working order.

Try It! **Reread the article to answer this question.**

In paragraph 2, the author says that cheese and yogurt are tasty foods. Is this detail important or not important? Why?

_____

_____

Read the poem. Use the Think About It to guide your reading. Then answer the question. Use the Hint to help you.

Think About It

The title gives an idea of what the poem is about. The details will tell what this means.

Hint

The question asks about Thursday. Look for the line in the poem about Thursday. What is the weather like that day?

A Whole Year in a Week

I once lived a whole year in a week.

On Monday it was spring, all cold and bleak.

On Tuesday there was sun, but it was still kind of cool.

By Wednesday it was summer, and we raced to the pool.

5   On Thursday it was even hotter—perfect for ice cream.

But on Friday it was fall, and fall is too short.

On Saturday it snowed, so we built a wonderful fort.

And then on Sunday I woke up. It had all been a dream!

In the poem, what season is it on Thursday?

A   spring

B   summer

C   fall

D   winter

CORRECT ANSWER The second answer choice is correct.

SUPPORTING DETAILS The fifth line says that on Wednesday it is summer. The next line says that on Thursday it is even hotter than on Wednesday.

INCORRECT ANSWERS The first answer choice is not correct because the poem's second line says that spring is on Monday.

The third answer choice is not correct because the poem's sixth line says that fall is on Friday.

The fourth answer choice is not correct because the poem's seventh line says that it snows on Saturday. That means that it is winter on Saturday.

New York   GPI/CPI 3.R.GPI.1e, 3.R.GPI.3a

Read the passage. Use each Think About It to guide your reading.

Bruno Takes a Walk

Think About It

Who is Ray? Who is Bruno? What are they doing?

Why does Ray need to be careful walking Bruno? Why does Ray tell Bruno that he is a good boy?

Where does Bruno run to? What do you think Ray is thinking when this happens?

Why does Bruno need quiet time?

1   One day after school, Ray decided to take his dog, Bruno, for a walk. Ray lived in a neighborhood with wide sidewalks and tall trees. He liked going out with Bruno. It helped him forget how loud it was at home with three sisters and two brothers. Every once in a while, Ray needed some quiet time.

2   Bruno, however, was a large dog. Well, he was large compared to Ray's mom and dad. Compared to little Ray, Bruno was huge! Ray needed to be very careful walking Bruno. After putting on his jacket, Ray wrapped the leash around his wrist three times. "Good boy," he said to Bruno.

3   As Ray and Bruno walked down the street, Bruno's head moved to the left. He smelled something. Ray tugged at Bruno's leash. "Good boy," he said to Bruno. "Good boy." Then Bruno's head moved to the right. *He must smell something else*, Ray thought. He tugged at the leash again. "Good boy," he said.

4   Then a squirrel suddenly dashed across a yard. Bruno let out a howl. The squirrel's brown tail stuck high in the air. Bruno took a great leap forward and ran.

5   The street was no longer quiet. Bruno barked and barked and barked. Ray yelled for him to stop, but it was hard to keep up with such a large dog. They passed tall trees and short bushes. They passed big houses and little garages. Lucky for Ray, the leash held on to Bruno. And Ray held on to the leash.

6   Finally, the squirrel scurried up a tree. Bruno barked, but he was tired. "Good boy," Ray said. He tossed Bruno a treat from his pocket. "Now you're the one who needs some quiet time!"

Hints

First, think about what the story is mostly about. Then, find the detail that tells the most about this main idea.

Reread the last paragraph of the story. To praise means to make someone feel good. What does Ray do to make Bruno happy?

Use the Hints to answer the questions below. Circle the letter for or write out each correct answer. Provide supporting details.

1   Which sentence is most important to the main idea of the story?

A   "Ray lived in a neighborhood with wide sidewalks and tall trees."

B   "It helped him forget how loud it was at home with three sisters and two brothers."

C   "Every once in a while, Ray needed some quiet time."

D   "After putting on his jacket, Ray wrapped the leash around his wrist three times."

Supporting Details: _____

_____

2   According to the story, what are the two things Ray does to praise Bruno? Use details from the story in your answer.

1. _____

_____

2. _____

_____

Hints

Look at paragraph 1. Why does Ray want to take Bruno for a walk? How does Bruno feel at the end of the story?

3 Why does Ray need some quiet time? When the walk is over, why is Bruno the one who needs quiet time? Use details from the story in your answer.

Why Ray needs quiet time: _____

_____

_____

_____

Why Bruno needs quiet time: _____

_____

_____

_____

What does Ray take on his walk with Bruno? Which of these items helps Ray the most?

4 What is probably most important for Ray to have while he is outside with Bruno?

A   a leash

B   a treat

C   a jacket

D   a brush

Supporting Details: _____

_____

PAIR SHARE

With your partner, share and discuss your answers and supporting details.

Directions
Read this article. Then answer questions 1 through 6.

The Queen of Jazz

by Riki Sheets

Ella Fitzgerald was born in Virginia in 1917. She soon moved to New York, where she spent the rest of her childhood. Life wasn't easy when Ella was young, but tough times helped make her into a great artist. In fact, she grew up to be the most popular jazz singer of all time.

Ella's family never had much money. Her stepfather dug ditches. Her mom cleaned other people's clothes for a living. Ella also helped the family by doing chores for her parents.

Ella Fitzgerald

Ella was always shy. Still, she made many friends in her neighborhood. She was a tomboy, which means that she liked playing with the boys as much as the girls. When the boys played baseball, she joined in. But Ella also loved music. She loved to dance to the records she found lying around her house. She moved her body however the music made her feel. Even when the music was sad, dancing made Ella happy.

Ella also liked to sing. She and her friends would turn on the radio and sing along with the songs they heard. When Ella was a girl, the music style we call jazz was new in America. It began in New Orleans, then moved to Chicago and New York. Many African Americans like Ella played jazz, but white musicians also began to play. Men mostly played the instruments, such as trumpet and saxophone. Women often sang the songs. Ella's favorite singers were three sisters called the Boswell Sisters.

Whenever she got a chance, Ella took a train to Harlem, New York. There, she went to the Apollo Theater. Singers and dancers played at the theater all the time. Sometimes, Ella would write her name on a piece of paper and put the paper in a hat. Each week, people drew names from the hat. The winners got to sing and dance at the Apollo! Ella was an amateur. That means that she had never been paid to sing or dance before. That was okay, though. On Amateur Night at the Apollo, no one else had been paid before, either.

One night when Ella was seventeen, her name was drawn at the Apollo. This was her chance to perform. She chose to dance. She loved to dance more than anything in the world. As she waited her turn, she watched the act before her. They were called the Edwards Sisters, and they danced, too. But Ella thought they danced much better than she did. "They were the dancingest sisters around," she said many years later.

Ella started to worry. Would the audience hate her because she could not dance like the Edwards Sisters? She thought about quitting. Then, at the last minute, Ella decided she would sing instead of dance.

She sang "Judy," her favorite song by the Boswell Sisters. She sang it with great feeling. She sang it with all the happiness and sadness of her childhood, and the crowd loved it. They yelled for her to sing another song. Ella's dancing days were over. She was about to become a singing star. She was about to become the Queen of Jazz.

1 Which word best describes Ella **right before** she sang at the Apollo Theater?

   A sad

   B happy

   C nervous

   D silly

2 What is the **most** important detail about Ella Fitzgerald in this article?

   A She liked to play baseball.

   B She had a difficult childhood.

   C She was born in Virginia.

   D She did chores for her parents.

3 According to the passage, which statement about jazz is true?

   A Only people in New Orleans played jazz.

   B Ella was the first great jazz musician.

   C Women usually played the instruments.

   D Jazz was new when Ella was a young girl.

4 The article says that Ella was

   A shy

   B rich

   C funny

   D beautiful

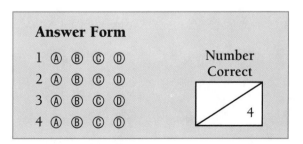

5 According to the article, what are the **two** ways that Ella Fitzgerald enjoyed music as a child? Use details from the article in your answer.

1. _____

_____

2. _____

_____

6 In the article, the author says that jazz was mainly played in three cities. Using details from the article, complete the web with the cities in which jazz was played. One has been done for you.

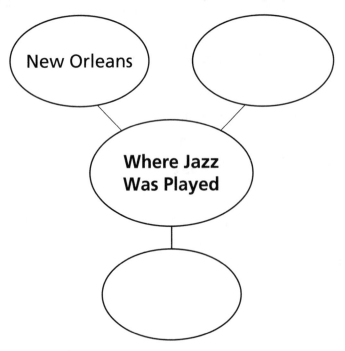

GPI/CPI

3.R.GPI.2h: Make predictions, draw conclusions, and make inferences

3.R.GPI.3c: Analyze ideas on the basis of prior knowledge

Introduction

Authors don't always tell you everything. For example, have you ever guessed what will happen next in a story? If so, you were making a prediction. A **prediction** is a type of guess about the future.

You can also draw conclusions. A **conclusion** is a decision you make by adding up facts. For example, pretend you walk outside one morning. You see puddles on the sidewalk. The grass and trees are wet, too. You can add up these facts to conclude that it rained in the night.

An inference is another type of guess. **Inferences** are ideas based on clues from the text. When you make an inference, you also think about what you already know. You make inferences every day. If you see smoke, you can guess there is a fire nearby. If you see someone smiling, you can guess that the person is happy. Sometimes, you can even add up inferences to draw conclusions and make predictions.

As you read, think about what the writer did not say. Then make a guess about the story, article, or poem. Make sure details from the text support this guess.

Use this chart to help you make guesses as you read.

Clues or Facts	What You Already Know	What You Figured Out

Read this story. Then answer the question below.

David's Daydream

1   I like to daydream. I like to imagine all kinds of things. On Tuesday, I had a daydream about reading minds. In this dream, my teacher knew that I felt good about the picture I drew. He asked me to tell the class about it. And the lunch lady could tell that I wanted fish sticks without my saying a word.

2   But then the daydream turned into a nightmare. Mom knew that I didn't like her haircut. And Jorge knew I didn't like the book he gave me. Maybe I should listen to what they've told me and stop all this daydreaming!

In the story, why does David's daydream most likely turn into a nightmare?

▶ In paragraph 1, what does David tell about? He tells about the good things that happen because people can read his mind.

▶ The first sentence of paragraph 2 says that the daydream becomes a nightmare. The paragraph supports that idea.

▶ How do you think David would feel if Mom and Jorge really knew how he felt? He would feel awful.

ANSWER: David's daydream turns into a nightmare because he sees how bad it would be for people to know some of his thoughts.

Try It!

Reread the story to answer this question.

From reading the story, you can tell that when David says "they" in the last sentence, he is probably talking about—

_____

Read the poem. Use the Think About It to guide your reading. Then answer the question. Use the Hint to help you.

Think About It

As you read, think about what it feels like to try something new. How does the mother help the little bird?

Hint

Use details and what you know about trying new things to make a prediction.

First Flight

The little red bird peeked out from her nest and
tried her best not to look down at the ground.
"It's time to fly," her mother chirped, and then
leapt into the great sky, her wings spread wide.
5   The little bird stepped closer to the edge,
and watched with hope as her mother flew.

What will most likely happen next in the poem?

A   The little bird will try to fly on her own.

B   The mother bird will bring the little bird food.

C   The little bird will choose to stay in the nest.

D   The mother bird will find a new home for her family.

CORRECT ANSWER   The first answer choice is correct.

SUPPORTING DETAILS   The title of the poem is "First Flight," and the mother bird tells the little bird that "it's time to fly."

INCORRECT ANSWERS   The second answer choice is not correct because the story does not talk about food the birds eat.

The third answer choice is not correct because the little bird steps closer to the edge of the nest. She also watches her mother "with hope." These clues mean that the little bird will probably try to fly.

The fourth answer choice is not correct because the poem gives no clues that the mother bird is looking for a home.

Read the story. Use each Think About It to guide your reading.

Making a Town with Mrs. Townsend

Think About It

Do you think the teacher is organized? How does she begin the project?

1   Mrs. Townsend stood in front of the class and said, "Today, we are going to make a town. We will think of all the things that a town needs, and then we will figure out how to make sure the town has these things. For example, a town needs a name. So we will make up a name for our town. Our town will need buildings, parks, and roads, so we will draw a map. Now, let's get started by listing as many things as we can think of that a town needs."

2   The teacher wrote the number 1 on the board at the front of the classroom. Next to the number, she wrote "a name." Then she said, "What else does a town need?" Lots of hands went up, and Mrs. Townsend called on Corbin.

3   "A town needs schools," said Corbin. Mrs. Townsend agreed and added that to the list. Then she called on another student, who said "stores." The next student said "a hospital," and the student after that said "firefighters." The list was growing.

Mrs. Townsend asks the class questions. Why do you think she does this?

4   Then Mrs. Townsend asked, "Who will deal with any crime in the town?" As soon as the students shouted out the answer, the teacher added it to the list. When she asked, "Where will the kids play?" the students called out, "Parks!" Very quickly, the class had a list of twenty things a town needs, including all types of people and places.

Where are the students going? After that, what will they probably do?

5   "Good work, students," said Mrs. Townsend. "Let's take a break, and when you come back inside, we will move on to the next step in this project."

Hints

Look at paragraph 1. There is a clue about what the next step in the project will be.

Look at paragraph 4. What answer do you think the class gives to Mrs. Townsend's question?

Look at the first and last paragraphs. Look for clues as to how the teacher has organized the town project.

PAIR SHARE

With your partner, share and discuss your answers and supporting details.

Use the Hints to answer the questions below. Circle the letter for each correct answer. Provide supporting details.

1   What will most likely happen next in the story?

A   The class will give their town a different name.

B   The class will get too busy to finish the project.

C   The class will begin working on a math project.

D   The class will figure out how to supply the town.

Supporting Details: _____

_____

2   What is the most likely reason Mrs. Townsend asks, "Who will deal with any crime in the town?"

A   She wants students to think of ways to stop crime.

B   She is starting the second part of the project.

C   She wants students to add "police" to the list.

D   She wants students to only name people.

Supporting Details: _____

_____

3   Which sentence about Mrs. Townsend is most likely true?

A   She is not excited to work on the town project.

B   She believes that projects should be broken into steps.

C   She wishes she knew more about what towns need.

D   She is worried that the list won't get finished today.

Supporting Details: _____

_____

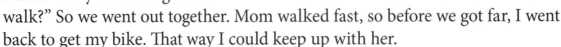

Directions
Read this story. Then answer questions 1 through 5.

Looking for Work

by Payton Orringer

My mom used to work at a car dealership that my uncle Jesse owns. But then one day she found out that she would need to get a different job. Jesse was selling the business. When Mom got home from work the day she learned the bad news, she walked around and around the apartment. She could not sit still.

"Are you okay, Mom?" I asked. She just nodded.

"It's such a nice night, Alea," said Mom. "Why don't we go for a walk?" So we went out together. Mom walked fast, so before we got far, I went back to get my bike. That way I could keep up with her.

We were gone for almost an hour, and the sun began to set. "Wow!" I said, pointing up at the sky.

"Bats!" Mom exclaimed. "Aren't they beautiful? I'm so glad we get to see so many bats at night." I agreed.

When we got home, Mom smiled and said, "Let's eat." She fixed dinner, the same as always. After dinner, she told me to do my chores, the same as always. Then she took out her laptop.

"I need to do some paperwork so I'll be ready to look for a new job. You head off to bed, but if I make too much noise, I want you to tell me."

Then she kissed me on the cheek and hugged me. She told me that everything would be okay. I have always thought that everything is okay, but when she said that, my stomach hopped a little. Why wouldn't everything be okay?

"Get up, sleepyhead!" Mom called the next morning. She was wide awake and dressed in her best suit. "I made pancakes for breakfast."

"Pancakes!" I cheered as I went into the kitchen. Usually I just eat cereal. "Are you going to have some, too?" I asked.

Mom didn't answer. She just walked around the apartment arranging things. She puffed up the couch pillows. She picked some dried leaves off a plant. Usually Mom and I eat breakfast together.

"Well, I went around to about twenty stores today," Mom said when she picked me up after school. "I had to fill out a lot of forms. They asked about where I went to school and what other jobs I'd had." She was quiet for a minute or two and then said, "It was a good day. Everything will be just fine."

When we got home, she said, "Let's go take a good long walk. Then when I fix dinner you can do your homework. We'll eat dinner in front of the TV. I'm too tired to talk much."

"If you're going to walk fast, I'll get my bike." I didn't say anything about eating in front of the TV. That was fine with me. Mom never lets me eat in front of the TV.

Every day for a month, Mom looked for work, and we took fast walks every evening. She kept saying that everything would be okay. I kept getting that hop in my stomach when she said it. But she was right. Everything is okay. Today my stomach did a different hop. Mom got a new job. Tonight we took a slow walk and laughed a lot.

1 Which sentence about Alea is **most likely** true?

  A Alea likes to go for walks with her mom.

  B Alea doesn't like to eat cereal.

  C Alea is afraid of bats flying.

  D Alea doesn't want her mom to get a job.

2 What **first** causes Alea's stomach to hop a little?

  A being hungry for pancakes

  B being worried about Mom

  C getting a stomachache

  D getting excited about taking a walk

3 At the end of the story, Alea **most likely** hopes that

  A she will get to eat in front of the TV

  B she won't have to do more chores

  C her mom will like her new job

  D her mom will work with Jesse again

4 What is the **most likely** reason Mom arranges things in the apartment?

  A She really wants the house to be clean.

  B She feels nervous about looking for a job.

  C She is trying to show Alea that everything is okay.

  D She feels rested after getting plenty of sleep.

5 Which sentence about Alea's mom is **most likely** true?

  A Walking is her favorite thing to do.

  B She didn't like working at the car dealership.

  C It is important that she have a job.

  D She wishes she didn't have to work at a job.

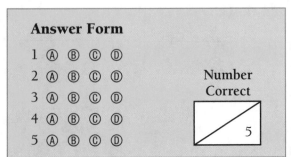

Answer Form

1 Ⓐ Ⓑ Ⓒ Ⓓ
2 Ⓐ Ⓑ Ⓒ Ⓓ
3 Ⓐ Ⓑ Ⓒ Ⓓ
4 Ⓐ Ⓑ Ⓒ Ⓓ
5 Ⓐ Ⓑ Ⓒ Ⓓ

Number Correct

/5

Introduction

Writers don't all write for the same reasons. People who write comic books want you to have fun. People who write school books want you to learn. And people who write ads want you to buy something.

A writer's reason for writing something is called the **author's purpose**. Here are some of the main purposes authors have when they write:

To inform: Sometimes, authors just want to help you learn more about something. Newspaper reporters write to inform, for example.

To entertain: Other times, writers want you to have fun. A person who writes a story about talking gorillas probably wants to entertain you.

To describe: Many times, people who write poems want to tell you what something feels, smells, sounds, looks, or tastes like. They want to tell about, or describe, the world.

To persuade: When writers persuade, they might tell you what you should think or feel about something. They might also try to get you to buy something. They sometimes use pictures and special words to help them meet their purpose.

Here is a chart you can use for finding the author's purpose:

Purpose	How I Know
to inform	uses lots of facts, is about real life
to entertain	sometimes made up, tells a good story
to describe	tells what things sound, look, feel, smell, and taste like
to persuade	uses words and pictures that show great feeling

Read this sign. Then answer the question below.

Camping Rules

1 Fires only in metal fire pits. Keep a bucket of water nearby.

2 No fishing without a state permit.

3 Campers under 18 years of age must be with a parent.

4 Pick up all trash before leaving. Place in large bins by the ranger station.

5 Cars and trucks on marked roads only.

6 Bicycles only on marked trails. No bicycles on foot trails.

What is the main purpose of this sign?

▶ Look at the rules on the sign. Who will read these rules? Campers will read the rules.

▶ What does the sign tell campers? It tells campers what they should and should not do while camping.

▶ Why did someone write these rules? The author wrote these rules to tell people how they should act when camping.

ANSWER: The main purpose of this sign is to give campers important information.

Try It!

Reread the sign to answer this question.

Where would you most likely find this sign?

_____

_____

©Curriculum Associates   Copying is not permitted.

Read the advertisement. Use the Think About It to guide your reading. Then answer the question. Use the Hint to help you.

Think About It

What is the ad about?
Who will see the ad?
What should these readers do?

Hint

What kind of information does the ad give?

Free Ice Cream!

This week only, buy one ice cream cone at Icy Jack's and get the second cone FREE! This offer is only good until Friday afternoon, so get yours while you can. Bring yourself, bring your friends, and bring your whole family!

Remember, at Icy Jack's you get the BEST ice cream at the BEST prices. Whatever your favorite kind of ice cream is, we have it! Hurry in to Icy Jack's before this great deal melts away forever.

This ad was written mainly to

A   invite readers to make their own ice cream.

B   ask readers to vote for their favorite ice cream.

C   get readers to buy ice cream at Icy Jack's.

D   get readers to give ice cream as a gift.

CORRECT ANSWER   The third answer choice is correct.

SUPPORTING DETAILS   The ad says, "buy one ice cream cone at Icy Jack's and get the second one FREE!" Readers must buy a cone before getting a free one.

INCORRECT ANSWERS   The first answer choice is not correct because the ad does not say anything about making ice cream.

The second answer choice is not correct because although the ad mentions readers' favorite ice cream, it does not ask them to vote on this.

The fourth answer choice is not correct because readers are asked to bring in family and friends, not to buy people ice cream as a gift.

Read the passage. Use each Think About It to guide your reading.

Think About It

Who do you think will read this newsletter? Who do you think wrote it?

Who is this next article about? Who would most want to learn this news?

What does this article tell about? Would the same people want to read this article?

The Gutierrez Gazette

Bouncing Baby Boys

The Gutierrez family is growing! Mark and Sonia became parents to Baby Enrique on April 7. Enrique weighed eight pounds and four ounces. Sean Gutierrez was born the next day. His parents are Carlos and Barb Gutierrez. Sean is their fourth child. He weighed six pounds, two ounces. Both boys are beautiful and healthy.

Gutierrez Gets Big Award

Evan Gutierrez finished four years at Northern College on May 10. He has a degree in math. He also received an award for being such a great student! Now, Evan has a new job in Denver. In a few years, he would like to go back to school. We are very proud of Evan.

Abuela Ella Turns Ninety-Five

Start baking cakes and making birthday cards! We're planning a huge party to celebrate our oldest and sweetest Gutierrez. Ella will be ninety-five in August. The party will be at the town park. We'll have music and games—fun for everyone. Mark your calendars for August 8. Ella wants to see you all! You can call, e-mail, or write to Barb Gutierrez to find out more. We'll also tell more about the party in the next *Gutierrez Gazette*.

PLEASE let us know if your e-mail or mailing address changes. We love sharing the *Gutierrez Gazette* and want to make sure we don't miss anyone!

Use the Hints to answer the questions below. Circle the letter for each correct answer. Provide supporting details.

1   Why did the author most likely write the articles in *The Gutierrez Gazette*?

   A   to ask family members to give money for a party

   B   to tell readers about each member of the Gutierrez family

   C   to entertain readers with a few interesting stories

   D   to tell about big things happening in the Gutierrez family

   Supporting Details: _____

   _____

2   Why did the author most likely write the second article?

   A   to tell people that Abuela's birthday is coming

   B   to tell people where Evan plans to go to school

   C   to find out who will be coming to Abuela's party

   D   to inform readers about why the family is proud of Evan

   Supporting Details: _____

   _____

3   Why does the author most likely tell readers to "start baking cakes"?

   A   to show how excited the family is about the new babies

   B   to show that Evan Gutierrez won a big award

   C   to show that a big party is coming up

   D   to show what Abuela Ella wants for her birthday

   Supporting Details: _____

   _____

PAIR SHARE

With your partner, share and discuss your answers and supporting details.

Directions
Read the passage. Then answer questions 1 through 5.

Making the List

by Maryann Walters

It was time for the Jones family to do their weekly food shopping. Mrs. Jones had all the kids helping her figure out what they needed. "This trip will be just for the basics," she said. "That means we will go around the outside of the store in a loop. We will just go to the produce, dairy, meat, and bakery sections. That will get us all we need." Then she added, "I like to break down my shopping list into smaller lists. Let me show you.

"First, let's see if we need any fruit or vegetables." She sent Stacy into the kitchen to see if they needed apples or oranges. They were out of apples, so Mrs. Jones put that on her list. They had three oranges, which would be enough for now. They also needed bananas, lemons, and grapes. Mrs. Jones said she would get raspberries for a treat.

Then the Joneses figured out what vegetables they needed. They needed lettuce, fresh spinach, onions, carrots, corn on the cob, and green beans. Mrs. Jones told the children, "I put all of the fruit and vegetables we need in a small list that is part of the big list. The small list is called Produce. All of those things are in the same part of the store. That's why I put them together on the list. This way we'll be sure to get everything we need."

Then Mrs. Jones said, "Next, I move around the outside of the store and come to the meat and dairy section. I know that we need milk. I need somebody to check if we have cottage cheese and cheese slices for sandwiches." Sally went to check. The Joneses needed cheese for sandwiches, but they had cottage cheese.

"What about butter?" Mrs. Jones asked. They needed butter, too. "This is going to be a long list," she said.

"Now what about meat? Shall we have fish this week?" All the children thought that was a great idea. "And shall we have our usual Meatloaf Monday?" Everybody liked that idea except for Mary, who didn't eat red meat. She would eat something else that night. Ground beef went on the list.

"Then we can have baked chicken one night, and I think that will be enough meat for the week." Now Mrs. Jones was thinking out loud. "We can have spaghetti with tomato sauce one night. And we can have some other meatless meals. Will somebody check for bread and tortillas?" They needed both. Here is what the final list looked like:

Produce		Dairy	Meat	Bakery
apples	lettuce	milk	fish	bread
bananas	spinach	cheese	ground beef	tortillas
grapes	onions	butter	chicken	
lemons	carrots			
raspberries	corn			
beans				

They were ready to go to the store, and it did not take long to shop with such a helpful list!

1 The author **most likely** wrote "Making the List" to

A help readers plan dinners for the week

B show readers how to work well together

C teach readers where foods are in a store

D tell readers a story about a family shopping

2 What is the **main** purpose of the list?

A to teach about food groups

B to show what the family will buy for meals

C to tell the store what to stock

D to make sure the kids eat healthy food

3 The author **most likely** wrote paragraph 1 to

A show readers how the kids help Mrs. Jones

B tell readers about the sections in the store

C let readers know that a shopping list is coming

D show readers what the family will eat

4 Why did the author **most likely** write the fourth paragraph?

A to tell what dairy products the family needs

B to give information about fruits and vegetables

C to tell readers that Mary doesn't eat red meat

D to give information about why milk is important

5 Why does the author **most likely** tell what Mrs. Jones plans to make for meals?

A to show how she comes up with the shopping list

B to show that the family likes eating meatless meals

C to show what the children can do to help with shopping

D to show why she wants to buy many kinds of fruit

Answer Form

1 Ⓐ Ⓑ Ⓒ Ⓓ
2 Ⓐ Ⓑ Ⓒ Ⓓ
3 Ⓐ Ⓑ Ⓒ Ⓓ
4 Ⓐ Ⓑ Ⓒ Ⓓ
5 Ⓐ Ⓑ Ⓒ Ⓓ

Number Correct

/5

Introduction

In this lesson, you will learn about facts and opinions. A **fact** is information that is true. It can be proved or checked. An **opinion** is what someone thinks, feels, or believes.

In writing, facts are usually clear. They can tell more about a person, place, thing, or event. For example, the sentence "Winter is colder than summer" is a fact. Facts can also tell what happened. The sentence "The Dillon Panthers won the game last Sunday" is another fact.

Be careful, though. Sometimes facts are wrong. They're still called facts, though. "Ants are larger than elephants" is still a fact even though it isn't true. That's because it can be proved wrong.

Opinions are people's ideas. They often begin with the words *I think* or *I believe*. Here are a few other clue words: *good*, *bad*, *best*, and *worst*. Sometimes opinions sound like facts. "Our cereal tastes best" is an opinion. It sounds true, but it is not. Not everyone would think it tastes best.

Most writing has both facts and opinions. Look for both as you read. The questions in the chart below can help you.

What is the statement?	Is it a fact?	Is it an opinion?	How do I know?
The Dillon Panthers won the game last Sunday.	✓		I can look in the newspaper.
Our cereal tastes best.		✓	the clue word *best*

Read this story. Then answer the question below.

Going to the Movies

1   "Hey, Dad!" Simon called. "Can I go to see *The Night of the Zombie Cats* with Jay? The movie is really scary, but it's rated okay for kids my age. Jay's parents are going, too."

2   "I don't think that's a good idea," Dad said. "You have school tomorrow. Also, remember how you felt when we watched that scary movie on TV last week? You were awake all night hearing strange bumps and crashes. You said you never wanted to watch another scary movie again!"

Which sentence in the first paragraph includes an opinion?

▶ What does Simon say first? He asks his dad if he can go see *The Night of the Zombie Cats* with Jay. That's a fact. He is asking if he can do something.

▶ Then what does Simon say? He says the movie is really scary but rated okay for kids his age. The movie rating is a fact. It can be proved. The movie being scary is an opinion. Some people might not think the movie is scary.

ANSWER: In the first paragraph, Simon gives the opinion that the movie *The Night of the Zombie Cats* is really scary.

Try It!

Reread the story to answer this question.

In the second paragraph, which statement is an opinion?

_____

_____

Read the advertisement. Use the Think About It to guide your reading. Then answer the question. Use the Hint to help you.

Think About It

What does the writer think about the cherries?

Hint

In ads, opinions often look like facts. Words like *best* and *worst*, *good* and *bad* are often hints that a statement is an opinion.

Cherries on Sale This Week

1   California cherries are on sale Thursday through Sunday this week. Stores sell these cherries for only a few weeks in the spring. California cherries are the best you can get, but they do spoil quickly. That's why you can't buy them all year long.

2   So remember to get cherries while you can. This is a wonderful fruit—wonderfully tasty and wonderfully healthy!

What sentence from the passage includes an opinion?

A   "California cherries are on sale Thursday through Sunday this week."

B   "Stores sell cherries for only a few weeks in the spring."

C   "That's why you can't buy them all year long."

D   "This is a wonderful fruit—wonderfully tasty and wonderfully healthy!"

CORRECT ANSWER   The fourth answer choice is correct.

SUPPORTING DETAILS   The word *wonderful* is a clue that this is an opinion. Some people might not think that cherries are wonderful and tasty.

INCORRECT ANSWERS   The first answer choice is not correct because this is a fact. You could call the store to check the days of the sale.

The second answer choice is not correct because it is a fact. You could check to see how long stores sell cherries for each spring.

The third answer choice is not correct because this is a fact that can be checked. You could find out whether you can buy California cherries all year long. You could also find out why this is so.

Read the passage. Use each Think About It to guide your reading.

Come to Nature Camp!

Think About It

Can you prove that the summer program is great? Can you prove that the camp has classes for kids in grades 1 through 6?

1   How do you plan to spend your summer vacation? If you want to have the best time ever and learn about nature, come to Goose Lake Camp. Goose Lake has a great summer program. The camp offers many different classes for kids in the first through sixth grades. Each class begins at eight o'clock every morning and ends at three o'clock in the afternoon. All of the classes last for one week and are held throughout the summer. The campers always have the best time they've ever had!

What does the writer think is a super class? What do the campers do in that class?

2   The camp has a super class called "A Week in the Woods" for third and fourth graders. Campers come on Monday. On that day, they learn the ABCs of camping in the woods. Then on Tuesday, they bring their sleeping bags and a bag packed with clothes. The campers hike into the woods and set up tents. For the rest of the week, they camp out. Every morning, they hike and learn cool facts about nature. Every night, they cook supper over a fire. The campers think the best part is the after-supper treat. They make the gooiest and most delicious s'mores.

What facts does the writer give about the class "What's Bugging You"?

3   "What's Bugging You?" is a class for campers of any age. It's about insects and spiders. Did you know that spiders are actually not insects? You'll learn why in this helpful and interesting class. Each day, campers will learn about—and even get a chance to hold!—a different kind of bug.

What does the writer think campers will do after just one week of camp?

4   If you want to learn about birds and bugs, plants and fish, and even about funny-looking frogs, sign up for Goose Lake Camp. Tell your friends to come, too. After just one week, you'll be begging your parents to sign you up for more classes!

Use the Hints to answer the questions below. Circle the letter for each correct answer. Provide supporting details.

1   Which sentence from paragraph 1 includes an opinion?

   A   "The campers always have the best time they've ever had!"

   B   "The camp offers many different classes for kids in the first through sixth grades."

   C   "Each class begins at eight o'clock every morning and ends at three o'clock in the afternoon."

   D   "All of the classes last for one week and are held throughout the summer."

Supporting Details: _____

_____

2   Which sentence from paragraph 2 does not include an opinion?

   A   "The camp has a super class called 'A Week in the Woods' for third and fourth graders."

   B   "Then on Tuesday, they bring their sleeping bags and a bag packed with clothes."

   C   "Every morning, they hike and learn cool facts about nature."

   D   "They make the gooiest and most delicious s'mores."

Supporting Details: _____

_____

3   Which sentence from paragraph 3 includes an opinion?

   A   "'What's Bugging You?' is a class for campers of any age."

   B   "It's about insects and spiders."

   C   "Did you know that spiders are actually not insects?"

   D   "You'll learn why in this helpful and interesting class."

Supporting Details: _____

_____

PAIR SHARE

With your partner, share and discuss your answers and supporting details.

Directions
Read the passage. Then answer questions 1 through 4.

The Best Pets Ever

by Hector Dejesus

Everybody should have a pet, and that pet should be a dog. Dogs make the most terrific pets in the world. Have you heard the saying "A dog is a person's best friend"? Well, it's true, because your dog will always be your best friend. There are many different breeds, or types, to choose from. Some breeds make better pets than others. Carefully choose the breed that will be best for you.

Working Dogs

Working dogs are one group of dogs. People raise and train them to work. Some guard and protect homes. Others pull sleds or save people from danger. Most working dogs are big and powerful. They need training and must get exercise every day. If you have a busy family, I think a dog from another group will be better for you.

A Great Dane is one kind of working dog. For the right family, Great Danes can be great pets. This breed is always friendly, but it is huge. In fact, it's over thirty inches tall—and that doesn't include its head! These gentle giants are much too big to live in a small apartment.

The Newfoundland is another big working dog. It is the sweetest working dog. If you like big, bear-like dogs, this is the breed of dog for you.

Newfoundland

Sporting Dogs

Sporting dogs are another group of dogs. These dogs love exercise and games. If your family spends a lot of time outdoors, these friendly dogs make amazing pets. Everybody who enjoys running should think about getting a sporting dog. It's a perfect running partner.

Labrador retrievers may be the most well-known sporting dog. Labradors once worked with fishermen, bringing in fishing nets. Some caught fish that got away from fishing lines. If you want a sporting dog, a Lab is the right dog to think about. Because they are retrievers, most Labs love to fetch. Throw a ball and they will chase after it and bring it right back. Some Labs will fetch for hours.

Toy Dogs

Many people like small dogs best. Some small dogs are called toy dogs. These tiny dogs love to spend time with their owners and sit on people's laps. If you live in a small apartment, a toy dog—such as a toy poodle—will fit right in.

Mixed-Breed Dogs

Some dogs are mixed breeds, or mutts. They are the friendliest dogs in the world. I love mixed breeds and believe they make the greatest pets. My two dogs are mixed breeds. Because they are a mix of Newfoundland and Labrador retriever, they are part working and part sporting dogs. They have the best parts of both! Mixed breeds are the only dogs for me, but whatever dog is right for you, then that's the dog to get. But do get a dog. It will be your best friend and your favorite pet.

1 Which sentence from the article includes a **fact**?

A "Everybody should have a pet, and that pet should be a dog."

B "Dogs make the most terrific pets in the world."

C "There are many different breeds, or types, to choose from."

D "It will be your best friend and your favorite pet."

2 According to the information in the article, which sentence is an **opinion**?

A People train working dogs to guard and protect people.

B Working dogs are not good for busy families.

C Most Great Danes are over thirty inches tall.

D Newfoundlands are large working dogs.

3 Which sentence about the article is an **opinion**?

A The author believes that owning a dog is a wise thing.

B The author tells about different kinds of dogs.

C The author owns two mixed-breed dogs.

D Some people call very small dogs toy dogs.

4 Which sentence from paragraph 6 includes an **opinion**?

A "Labradors once worked with fishermen, bringing in fishing nets."

B "Some caught fish that got away from fishing lines."

C "If you want a sporting dog, a Lab is the right dog to think about."

D "Throw a ball and they will chase after it and bring it right back."

Answer Form

1 Ⓐ Ⓑ Ⓒ Ⓓ
2 Ⓐ Ⓑ Ⓒ Ⓓ
3 Ⓐ Ⓑ Ⓒ Ⓓ
4 Ⓐ Ⓑ Ⓒ Ⓓ

Number Correct

4

Lesson 7
Organizational and Text Features

GPI/CPI

3.R.GPI.1f: Recognize and use organizational features

3.R.GPI.1g: Use text features to understand informational texts

Introduction

In this lesson, you will learn about tools writers use to make meaning clear.

Organizational features help show how writers put ideas together. Here are a few organizational features you might see in books:

Chapter headings: These tell what each section of a book is about.

Table of contents: This lists the names and page numbers for all the chapters in a book. It comes at the beginning of a book.

Index: This comes at the end of a book. It lists important words from the book and shows you what page to turn to in the book to learn more about those words.

Text features help readers "see" and understand what the writer is saying. Here are a few text features:

Pictures include maps, drawings, and more.

Captions tell what is happening in a picture.

Charts and graphs show facts and ideas clearly.

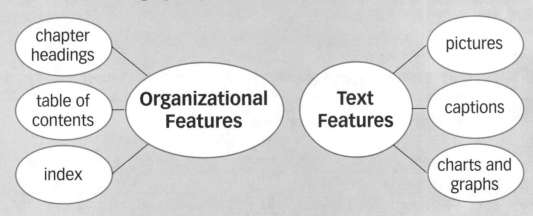

Read this article. Then answer the question below.

How Glass Is Made

1   Glass is made naturally when lightning strikes sand. The heat of the lightning melts the sand. The heat from volcanoes makes glass, too. The heat melts rocks and sand together.

2   People make glass by mixing sand with other materials. Everything is then melted together to make a thick liquid. When the liquid cools, it hardens into glass. But while it is hot, the liquid is made into useful things. It is pressed to make items like dishes. It can also be blown into shapes.

What can you learn from the article's title?

▶   What is the title of this article? The title is "How Glass Is Made."

▶   What does a title often tell? The title often tells what a passage is going to be about.

▶   What is the rest of the passage about? It tells how glass is made.

▶   Does the title match the rest of the passage? Yes. The title tells what the article is about.

ANSWER: You can learn the article's main idea from the title.

Reread the article to answer this question.

How does the author arrange ideas in the article?

_____

_____

Read the story. Use the Think About It to guide your reading. Then answer the question. Use the Hint to help you.

Think About It

As you read, ask yourself what the story is mostly about.

Hint

What often goes with stories to help readers see what is happening?

Stuck on the Water

Zach and his mother sat in the small sailboat. There was no wind, so the sails didn't flap even a little bit. Zach wondered if his mom should try the motor again, but he didn't ask. She had tried several times and it wouldn't start. How would they get home? Would they be out on the lake all night? They hadn't seen another boat for hours. Zach looked toward shore, where his mom was suddenly pointing. They both began laughing as they watched a boat head their way.

What would most help a reader better understand the story?

A   a map of the lake Zach and his mother are on

B   a chart showing different kinds and sizes of boats

C   a drawing of Zach and his mother in the sailboat

D   an index listing important words from the story

CORRECT ANSWER   The third answer choice is correct.

SUPPORTING DETAILS   The passage is a made-up story. Often, drawings help readers see what characters look like, where they are, and what they are doing.

INCORRECT ANSWERS   The first answer choice is not correct because the story is not about the lake. It is about two characters who are stuck on their boat.

The second answer choice is not correct because the story doesn't tell about different kinds of boats. That is not the story's focus.

The fourth answer choice is not correct because an index usually goes at the end of a book, not a short story.

Think About It

Look at the title. It tells what the passage is about.

The words in **bold** are important. They are darker than the other words. How do they help you?

Can you picture a color wheel in your mind? What might help you see what the author is telling about?

Read the passage. Use each Think About It to guide your reading.

The Color Wheel

1   A color wheel looks like a pie, with colors as the pieces. The wheel shows how the colors are like or unlike one another.

2   **Primary colors.** The primary colors are red, yellow, and blue. You can't make these three colors by mixing other colors. Red, yellow, and blue are evenly spaced on the wheel.

3   **Secondary colors.** The secondary colors are orange, green, and purple. You make these colors by mixing two primary colors. Mixing red and yellow makes orange. That is why orange is between red and yellow on the color wheel. Mixing yellow and blue makes green. That's why green goes between yellow and blue on the wheel. Mixing blue and red makes purple, which is between those two primary colors.

4   **Tertiary colors.** Other colors are tertiary colors. You make these colors by mixing one primary and one secondary color. Yellow-orange is a tertiary color. To make it, you mix yellow (primary) and orange (secondary). On the color wheel, yellow-orange is between yellow and orange. Another tertiary color is blue-green. To make it, mix together blue and green. On the wheel, blue-green is between blue and green.

5   **Using a color wheel.** You can use a color wheel to see which colors look good together. Suppose you are picking out paint colors for a room. Do you want the colors to stand out? Choose colors that are opposite each other on the wheel. Do you want the room colors to match? Choose colors next to each other. In the same way, you can use the wheel when picking what to wear and what colors to use in an art project. It's a handy tool!

Hints

Reread the headings, or the **bold** words. What do those words tell about?

What colors from the article are in the picture?

Use the Hints to answer the questions below. Circle the letter for each correct answer. Provide supporting details.

1 Why does the author put some words in bold?

A to tell what each paragraph is about

B to show when someone is speaking

C to show which colors are most important

D to tell different ways to use the color wheel

Supporting Details: _____

_____

2 What does this picture show?

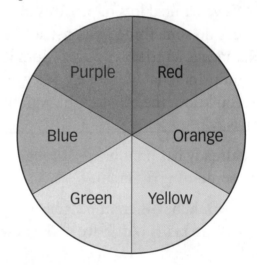

A primary colors only

B primary and secondary colors

C primary and tertiary colors

D all of the colors on the color wheel

Supporting Details: _____

_____

PAIR SHARE

With your partner, share and discuss your answers and supporting details.

Directions
Read this story. Then answer questions 1 through 5.

THE PROBLEM WITH PAW PRINTS

by Shirley Range

The Junaid kids wanted to make their mom something for her birthday. "I think we should paint some pictures," Shakeel said.

Shakeel's older sister, Nadia, shook her head. "We've painted lots of pictures for Mom. Let's do something new instead," she said. Nadia was a little bit bossy. "Mom loves those handprints that we made for her out of clay. You know, the ones on the wall in the stairway."

"She already has handprints, though," Shakeel said. "I thought you wanted us to do something different."

"They would be different because we're bigger now," Nadia replied. "Those handprints are really old. If we make new ones, Mom can see how we've grown."

"Well," Shakeel said slowly, "okay."

Just then their new puppy, Fred, walked through the room. Fred was white with brown spots, and he was a big and very silly puppy. "I know," Shakeel said in an excited voice, "let's make paw prints instead of handprints! We can do prints for both Fred and for Sasha." Sasha was their old cat who usually liked to be left alone.

"There's only one problem," said Nadia. "How are we going to get animals to make clay paw prints?"

"We'll use paint instead," Shakeel smiled. And he went off to get his paints.

They grabbed Sasha and Fred and went into the kitchen. Nadia put some paint on a plate. "Let's start with Sasha," she said. Sasha almost seemed to like making her prints. "It's like she's done this before," Nadia said. She let the cat go free and painted the word *Sasha* under the paw prints.

"Uh-oh!" cried Shakeel, pointing to a path of Sasha-prints that went all the way into the living room. "We'll have to clean that up when we're done."

Fred was jumping all around in his puppy way, so Shakeel held a dog treat above his nose. While Fred looked at the treat, Nadia tried to put paint on a front paw. Fred's paw landed hard in the plate of paint. Paint splashed everywhere. It got on Nadia's shirt and on the top of the stove. "Now you're spotted like Fred!" Shakeel said to Nadia, laughing.

The children got another treat and tried again. This time, Fred had to lie down for the treat. They got a paw print just before he jumped up and raced toward the living room. He left a trail of really big paw prints next to Sasha's tiny ones.

The painted paw prints washed easily from the kitchen floor but never completely washed out of the living room rug. The kids were worried about it, but Mom didn't care. She loved her present. And she loved seeing Fred and Sasha's "hands" hanging in the stairway next to Nadia's and Shakeel's.

Painted Prints

1. First, you will need a strong, thick sheet of paper and some paint. (Make sure it is paint you can wash off your hand when you're done.)

2. Pour some paint on a plate.

3. Press the palm of your hand into the paint. Be sure your whole palm is covered in paint.

4. Press the palm with paint on it onto the paper for about 10 seconds.

5. Allow plenty of time for the paint to dry.

---

1 You can tell from the picture on page 60 that

A Shakeel is taller than Nadia

B Nadia is taller than Shakeel

C clay paw prints are hard to make

D the paw prints won't wash off

2 What information can be found in the section "Painted Prints"?

A how Mom felt about the prints

B how clay prints are different from painted prints

C directions for making prints

D directions for getting paw prints from pets

3 According to "Painted Prints," what kind of paper is **best** to use?

A large and dark

B small and white

C think and light

D strong and thick

4 What can you learn from the story's title?

A that Mom's birthday is coming up

B that something goes wrong

C what Mom wants for her birthday

D what kinds of pets the family has

5 What would **most** help a reader better understand the story?

A a picture of the finished paw prints

B a caption for the picture on page 60

C a map of the Junaids' neighborhood

D a chart showing the Junaids' pets

Answer Form

1 Ⓐ Ⓑ Ⓒ Ⓓ

2 Ⓐ Ⓑ Ⓒ Ⓓ

3 Ⓐ Ⓑ Ⓒ Ⓓ

4 Ⓐ Ⓑ Ⓒ Ⓓ

5 Ⓐ Ⓑ Ⓒ Ⓓ

Number Correct

/5

Lesson 8
Graphic Organizers

GPI/CPI

3.R.GPI.1l: Use graphic organizers to record details from informational texts

3.R.GPI.2m: Use graphic organizers to record story details

Introduction

In this lesson, you will learn how to make pictures about what you read. You can use pictures for any kind of writing, from stories to poems to articles. These pictures are called graphic organizers. **Graphic organizers** help you arrange ideas. This makes these ideas easy to remember and use.

Some pictures are charts that show the order things happen in a story or article. These are sometimes called **sequence charts** or **story maps**. Here is an example of a sequence chart:

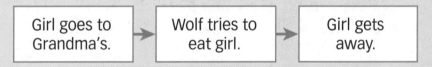

| Girl goes to Grandma's. | → | Wolf tries to eat girl. | → | Girl gets away. |

Other charts help you keep track of details.

What Girl Looks Like
young
red cloak

Sometimes, you can use **webs** to keep track of details as well.

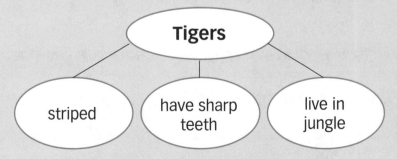

Read this passage. Then answer the question below.

Lots of Language

1   Mrs. Solon works hard. She has twenty-five kids in her class. Those kids speak four different languages. All of them speak English, but some speak another language at home. Pierre, for example, speaks French at home.

2   One day, Mrs. Solon wrote down all of the languages the students speak. Twenty-five students speak English. Ten kids speak Spanish, and five kids (including Pierre) speak other languages. That is quite a mix!

Look at this chart about languages in Mrs. Solon's class.

What Students Speak in Mrs. Solon's Class

English	25 students
Spanish	?
?	5 students

What phrase best fits in the first empty box?

▶ Look at the first row. How many students speak English? 25 students

▶ Look at the second row and at the passage. How many students speak Spanish? 10 students

ANSWER: The second row should say "10 students."

Try It!

Reread the passage to answer this question.

What phrase best fits in the second empty box?

_____

Read the passage. Use the Think About It to guide your reading. Then answer the question. Use the Hint to help you.

Think About It

What does Justin want to buy?

Hint

Look at the oval that has been filled in. Then reread the passage. What two things are listed in the passage that aren't yet on the web?

Mowing Money

Justin made some money mowing lawns, and he thought about how to spend it. He wanted to rent a movie. He also wanted a new baseball. Finally, he wanted an action figure.

Complete the web below with two things Justin plans to spend money on. One oval has been filled in for you.

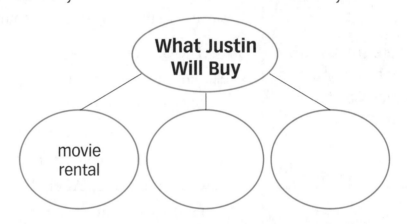

CORRECT ANSWER   The correct answers are "new baseball" and "action figure."

SUPPORTING DETAILS   The center bubble of the web is called "What Justin Will Buy." This means that the other bubbles should list the different things that Justin will spend his money on.

In the second sentence of the passage, Justin wants to rent a movie. Because of this, "movie rental" is one of the bubbles in the web.

In the third sentence, Justin wants a new baseball. In the last sentence, the author says that Justin also wants an action figure.

Read the article. Use each Think About It to guide your reading.

One Big Storm

Think About It

Read the first paragraph carefully. It helps you know what the rest of the article is about.

What are some of the facts the author tells about the Great Red Spot?

How is the Great Red Spot different today than it was 100 years ago? How will it be different in the future?

1   You know that storms happen all the time all over the world. We have snowstorms, windstorms, rainstorms, and even sandstorms! Did you know that other planets have storms, too? Many of these storms are larger and last longer than any storm here on Earth. The planet Jupiter's biggest storm is called the Great Red Spot. This storm is so big and so strong that Earth storms seem pretty small in comparison.

2   The Great Red Spot got its name from both its size and color. The storm is so big that you can see it in many pictures of Jupiter. It's big enough to fit two or three Earths inside of it. Also, the storm is oval-shaped, and it's a deep red color. Scientists think the storm may get its color from the materials it digs up from deeper down on the planet. After all, winds in the storm are up to 300 miles per hour!

3   Jupiter's storm is great and red. It's also been around for a long time. Most Earth storms last only a few hours or a couple of days. But the Great Red Spot is probably up to 300 years old.

4   Although the Great Red Spot is old, it does seem to change over time. For example, pictures of Jupiter from around 100 years ago show a Great Red Spot that is much longer than what we see today. Scientists believe that the spot might be closer to a circle by the year 2040.

5   The storm may change, but it is probably not going away anytime soon. The next time you're waiting for a rainstorm to pass so you can play outside, think about Jupiter. If you lived inside the Great Red Spot, you'd have a long wait!

Hints

Remember what the article is mostly about. Then go back to the article and find details that support this idea.

Use the Hints to answer the questions below. Circle the letter for or write in each correct answer. Provide supporting details.

1. In this article, the author gives many details about the Great Red Spot. Complete the chart with words that tell about the Great Red Spot. One box has been filled in for you.

Great Red Spot

red in color

Reread paragraph 2 in the article. What shape does the author say the Great Red Spot has today?

2. The chart below shows how the Great Red Spot is changing over time.

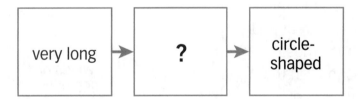

Which step best belongs in the empty box?

A   square-shaped

B   triangle-shaped

C   oval-shaped

D   star-shaped

Supporting Details: _____

_____

Hints

The chart tells you that the article is about the Great Red Spot. Which phrase best tells about this spot?

3 Read the chart below.

What "The Great Red Spot" Is About

where the spot is located
?
how old the spot is

Which phrase best completes the chart?

A when the spot will disappear

B how the spot is like a sandstorm

C people who have studied the spot

D how the spot got its name

Supporting Details: _____

_____

What details does the author give to tell about the Great Red Spot? Use these details to fill in the empty parts of the web.

4 Complete the web below with two facts about the Great Red Spot. One oval has been filled in for you.

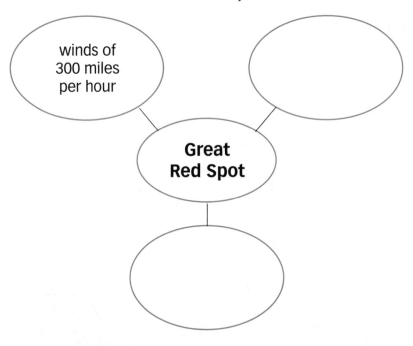

PAIR SHARE

With your partner, share and discuss your answers and supporting details.

GPI/CPI 3.R.GPI.1l, 3.R.GPI.2m   New York

Directions
Read this story. Then answer questions 1 through 4.

Mother's Day Breakfast

by Wilson Eilers

When I went downstairs this morning, Dad was already in the kitchen. "Shhh," he said. "Don't wake Mom. Let's get Rachel and make some breakfast." Just then, Rachel burst into the kitchen, looking wide awake and very happy.

"I'm hungry!" she said in a cheerful voice. Dad reminded us then that it was Mother's Day and that he wanted the three of us to give Mom a special treat. He wanted us to make her breakfast in bed.

"But first, let's feed you two." So Dad cut some oranges and made some toast with peanut butter. While we were eating, he said, "What should we make for Mom?"

"Pancakes and french toast!" I said.

"Good idea," he said, "but let's do just one or the other. How about pancakes with some sliced fruit and eggs?"

"I want some sliced fruit, too," Rachel said.

"Sure, Rachel. We'll make enough for all of us. Now, let's see. Will you get a pan for the pancakes and another one for the eggs?"

We got the pans out, and Dad got a bowl for the pancake batter. He mixed the batter, and we helped by getting out the milk, butter, eggs, and flour.

"We'll cook the pancakes first," Dad said, using his teacher voice. When the pan was hot, he poured in spoonfuls of batter. He then began cracking eggs in a big bowl.

"Let's go ahead and make a few pancakes for us so that Mom can sleep a bit longer, okay?" Dad asked.

So, Dad put three small pancakes on a plate for each of us. Because we are twins, we are very careful that things stay even and fair. We ate the pancakes while Dad kept Mom's pancakes warm in one pan and began cooking the eggs in the other.

After a moment, he said, "The eggs looks ready. Rachel, can you grab another plate to put over the egg pan to keep it warm?" She did that while Dad sliced up a pineapple and a few strawberries. Those pieces of fruit looked and smelled so good I couldn't help but stare.

Dad smiled at me. "You're looking at that pineapple like a hungry little puppy, Lisa. Don't worry. We'll all have some as soon as I cut up the rest of it." He grabbed a tray out of the cupboard and asked what we thought Mom would like to drink.

"Coffee," Rachel said, "and milk and juice."

"Everything?" Dad said. "Okay, since it's Mother's Day. Can you girls find the cards you made?"

We did that, and when we came back to the kitchen, Dad had the tray ready. At last, it was time to go wake Mom.

We went up the stairs and into Mom and Dad's room, where Mom was pretending to be asleep and snoring. "Surprise!" we yelled. And then we all sat on the bed and dug into one big and tasty Mother's Day breakfast.

1 The chart below shows the steps for making pancakes.

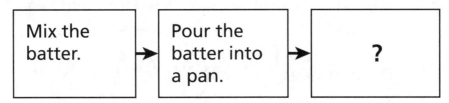

| Mix the batter. | → | Pour the batter into a pan. | → | ? |

Which sentence belongs in the empty box?

A Put the pancakes on a plate.

B Heat up the pancake pan.

C Mix milk, butter, eggs, and flour.

D Put a plate over the pancake pan.

2 The chart below shows what happens in the story. Complete the chart, using details from the story.

WHAT HAPPENS IN THE STORY

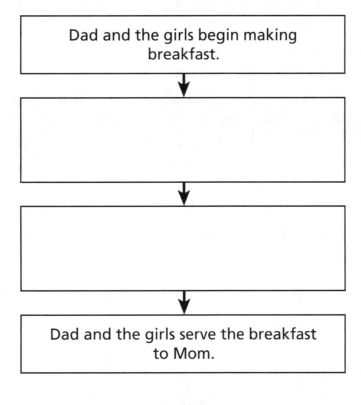

Dad and the girls begin making breakfast.

↓

↓

↓

Dad and the girls serve the breakfast to Mom.

Answer Form

1 Ⓐ Ⓑ Ⓒ Ⓓ

3 In the story, Dad and the girls make three kinds of food. Using details from the story, complete the web with the things Dad and the girls make for Mom. One has been done for you.

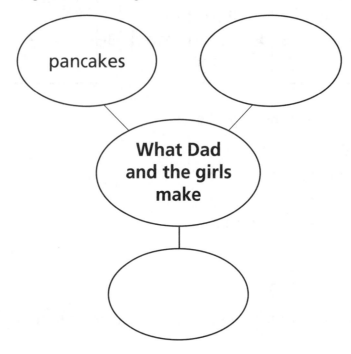

4 The chart below shows what Rachel does in the story.

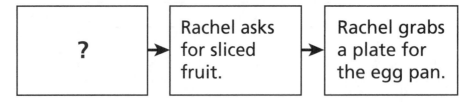

Which sentence **best** belongs in the empty box?

A Rachel says "I'm hungry!" in a happy voice.

B Rachel pretends to be asleep and snoring.

C Rachel eats three small pancakes.

D Rachel tells Dad what day it is.

Answer Form

4 Ⓐ Ⓑ Ⓒ Ⓓ

GPI/CPI

3.R.GPI.2f: Explain the difference between fact and fiction

3.R.GPI.3a: Evaluate the content by identifying realistic elements

Introduction

You probably already know that there are different kinds of writing. Here are some of the main kinds:

- **Nonfiction** tells about things that are true. (For example, many articles give facts.) It also tells about the world we live in. A nonfiction article might tell how the human body works or what's in space.

- **Fiction** tells stories that are made up. In fiction, the author thinks up people or animals and then tells what happens to these characters. The author also tells where and when these things happen.

- **Poetry** is a special kind of writing. Many poems have line breaks in them. Sometimes, the last words in different lines rhyme, but not always. Poets often write poems to tell what the world looks and feels like for them. Poems can be made up, or they can tell about real life.

Even though fiction is made up, it can still tell about people, places, and things that are realistic. If something is **realistic**, it could happen or be real. For example, a story about a boy who goes to school is realistic. That's because that story could happen in real life. Other stories are different. A story about a monkey who gets good grades at school is not realistic at all!

Think about the difference between fact and fiction when you read.

| made-up story | + | world like our own | = | realistic |

Read this story. Then answer the question below.

The First Game

1   At the start of Peter's first game, he climbed the pitcher's mound. The coach watched closely. Peter's parents sat in lawn chairs. They clapped and cheered. The batter dug in at home plate. He patted his helmet and scowled.

2   Peter leaned over and got the sign from the catcher. He pitched the ball 500 miles per hour! That was hundreds of miles faster than anyone had ever pitched before. Well, that's what Peter hoped would happen, anyway. Who knew? After taking one last look at Mom, Dad, and Coach, he threw the ball.

Which sentence tells something that could not really happen?

▶ Reread the passage. As you read, ask yourself, "Could this happen in real life?" Most of the sentences tell about things that could happen.

▶ As you think about each event, remember: If it could happen, then it is realistic. If it could not happen, then it is not realistic.

▶ Is it realistic for a boy to pitch in a baseball game? Yes, it is. Is it realistic for his mom and dad to cheer him on? Yes, it is. Is it realistic for a boy to pitch "hundreds of miles faster than anyone had ever pitched before"? No, it isn't.

ANSWER: A boy pitching a baseball 500 miles per hour could not happen.

Try It!

Reread the story to answer this question.

Is it realistic for the coach to watch Peter closely? Why or why not?

_____

_____

Read the poem. Use the Think About it to guide your reading. Then answer the question. Use the Hint to help you.

Think About It

Ask yourself what in the poem could happen in the real world.

Hint

Look at the last two lines of the poem. What happens?

Miss Kitty and the Mouse

Last night I dreamt about my cat,
So happy purring in my lap.
But then she spied a mouse on the floor
And watched it run to the front door.
5   Miss Kitty jumped, tail high in the air,
But the tiny mouse didn't give a care.
"Catch me!" it squeaked. "What's your excuse?"
Miss Kitty sighed and said, "Oh, what's the use!"

Which idea from the poem could not really happen?

A   a person dreaming

B   a cat purring

C   a mouse running

D   a mouse talking

CORRECT ANSWER   The fourth answer choice is correct.

SUPPORTING DETAILS   The mouse runs across the floor. He looks at the cat. Then he talks. He says, "Catch me!" In the real world, mice can't talk.

INCORRECT ANSWERS   The first answer choice is not correct because in the real world, people can dream. Most people dream every night.

The second answer choice is not correct because in the real world, cats purr to show that they are happy or upset.

The third answer choice is not correct because mice run all the time in the real world.

Think About It

Read the title first. What do you think this passage will be about? What is a "case"?

Who is this passage about? What are the sisters like?

How does Gladys solve the case? Who has taken the toothpaste?

Read the passage. Use each Think About It to guide your reading.

The Case of the Missing Toothpaste

1   Gladys and Margo were sisters. "I didn't do it!" Gladys would say whenever anything happened. "You did, too!" Margo would say right back. When the sun came up, Margo yawned and said, "Good morning, Gladys." And Gladys replied, "I didn't do it!"

2   "You did, too!" Margo said.

3   This was how the sisters were.

4   Then one night before bed, something happened. "Where is the toothpaste?" Margo barked. "I didn't do it!" Gladys said.

5   "Then who did?" Margo asked.

6   The sisters decided to find out what happened.

7   They stood in the bathroom with their arms crossed. For once, they were quiet as they looked around. The sound of the sink dripping was the only noise in the room. *Drip . . . drip . . .*

8   "I did it!" Gladys cried finally.

9   "I knew it!" Margo said, shaking a finger at her sister.

10   But Gladys told her sister that she hadn't meant that she herself had taken the toothpaste. Instead, she meant that she had solved the mystery. She knew where the toothpaste was.

11   Gladys pointed to the bathroom sink. She showed her sister the puddles of water on the counter and the paw prints leading out of the bathroom. Then they followed the tracks down the hall. The tracks led to a closet, which the girls opened. "Aha!" they both said. And there was their dog Stu happily brushing his teeth.

12   "Just as I thought," Gladys said.

Hints

Think about whether each sentence tells about the world we live in.

What kind of writing tells what characters do to solve a problem?

Think about what Margo does in the story. How is she different from Gladys?

Use the Hints to answer the questions below. Circle the letter for each correct answer. Provide supporting details.

1   Which sentence tells something that could not really happen?

A   A dog brushes its own teeth.

B   A young girl eats toothpaste.

C   Two sisters argue with each other.

D   Two sisters find their dog in a closet.

Supporting Details: _____

_____

2   This passage is most like a

A   poem

B   news story

C   made-up story

D   history article

Supporting Details: _____

_____

3   According to the passage, which statement about Margo is true?

A   She solves the case.

B   She is wrong about Gladys.

C   She takes the toothpaste.

D   She always says, "I didn't do it!"

Supporting Details: _____

_____

Directions
Read this passage. Then answer questions 1 through 5.

Back Home

by Spencer Norris

Beginning at seven thirty, the bedroom lights slowly switched on. The lights were supposed to look like the sun rising, so they did not come on all at once. The pretend daylight seemed to shine on Jackson's dreams. This morning, he was dreaming of the sun. He had never actually seen it, but he had heard many stories. People said that the sun was a beautiful, glowing yellow ball. It was far, far away from where Jackson was now. It was all the way over by Earth! Finally awake, Jackson slowly opened his eyes.

Jackson's sister, Polly, stood above him. Her hands were on her hips. "Mom wants us to be ready at nine o'clock," she said. "You do remember about the surprise, don't you?"

"What surprise?" Jackson mumbled. He was trying not to yawn.

"What surprise?" Polly said, her voice rising. "The surprise Mom promised us, of course! She told us to be ready at nine for a surprise. You've got to get ready!"

Jackson looked at the clock. It was now eight thirty. He liked to sleep in on Saturdays. During the week, school tired him out.

Jackson and his sister had lived on the spaceship their whole lives. Their parents had lived on the ship their whole lives, too. On the ship's main deck, workers were building a stage for next week's big celebration. It was going to be the 100th anniversary of the ship leaving Earth. It left back in the year 2020.

Jackson learned about those days in his history class. He wondered what it was like to use the Internet. Or ride in a car. Jackson couldn't picture what it would be like to use a steering wheel. He was so used to whooshing through space.

Whenever Jackson asked Polly what she thought about Earth, she rolled her eyes. "Who cares about Earth?" she said. "I like it here, on the ship. This is our home, after all."

It was now about twenty minutes before nine. Jackson shuffled into the bathroom to clean his teeth. He opened his mouth wide in a forced smile. It always felt to him like a school picture that lasted too long. A rush of air shot from behind the sink, and the air cleaned his teeth. It was much easier than brushing.

When he walked into the kitchen, Polly was already done with breakfast. Jackson slouched in his chair. After a minute's silence, Polly said, "Fine. I'll make you some french toast."

"Really?" Jackson said. He loved real french toast instead of the toast that came from their computer.

"What do you think the surprise will be?" Polly said as she cracked an egg in a bowl.

Jackson thought hard. Would Mom bring them a flower from the ship's greenhouse? Would she get them a new robot puppy?

Then, suddenly, the kitchen doors opened.

"My dears," Mom said with a big, clean smile, "we're going home. We're going back to Earth!"

Jackson gave a happy cheer, but Polly frowned. "Well, that's just great," she said.

1 This passage is **most** like a

A science-fiction story
B real-life story
C science article
D poem

2 Which sentence tells something that could **not** really happen?

A A boy dreams of the sun and Earth.
B A boy wakes up and cleans his teeth.
C A boy eats french toast for breakfast.
D A boy lives his whole life in space.

3 According to the passage, which statement about Jackson and Polly's parents is true?

A They have never been to Earth.
B They were born on Earth.
C They teach in the ship's school.
D They know how to drive cars.

4 According to the passage, which statement about life on the spaceship is true?

A All food comes from computers.
B Flowers grow in the greenhouse.
C The ship flies around a new sun.
D People ride around the ship in cars.

5 Complete the web below with **two** things that were once used on Earth but are no longer used on the spaceship.

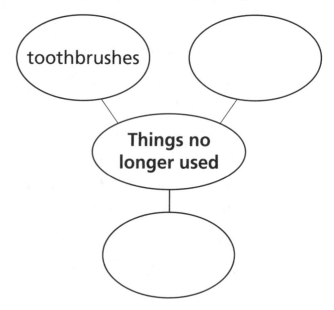

toothbrushes

Things no longer used

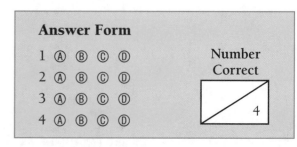

Answer Form

1 Ⓐ Ⓑ Ⓒ Ⓓ
2 Ⓐ Ⓑ Ⓒ Ⓓ
3 Ⓐ Ⓑ Ⓒ Ⓓ
4 Ⓐ Ⓑ Ⓒ Ⓓ

Number Correct

4

Lesson 10
Finding Information

GPI/CPI

3.R.GPI.1b: Read unfamiliar texts to collect data, facts, and ideas

3.R.GPI.1d: Locate information in a text that is needed to solve a problem

Introduction

In this lesson, you will learn about finding different kinds of information in a passage. You also will learn how to go back over a passage to find what you need to know.

Facts are bits of information. Male ladybugs are smaller than females. That's a fact. **Data** are facts that have been gathered together. A Web site might have data about ladybugs. It might tell how big ladybugs are, what they eat, and more. **Ideas** help you understand facts. Female ladybugs are bigger than males for a reason. That's an idea.

Sometimes, you need to go back and find information in a passage. Finding key words can help. **Key words** are the most important words that tell about what you are reading. For example, if you are reading about how big ladybugs are, *ladybug* and *size* might be key words.

Imagine you are reading about birds. Here is a question you might have:

What is the national bird of the United States?

The key words are *national*, *bird*, and *United States*. If you looked for these words in the passage, you would probably learn that the national bird of the United States is the bald eagle.

What is my question?	What are the key words?	What is the answer?
What is the national bird of the United States?	*national, bird, United States*	bald eagle

Read this article. Then answer the question below.

Living in Tough Places

1   Camels live in the desert. All animals need food and water. They also need to keep cool. The desert is hot and dry. There is little to eat. Still, camels eat and drink their fill. They are furry, yet they stay cool. How do they do that?

2   Camels store water in their humps. They can walk for miles to find a drink, and they can go days without a sip of water. They will eat anything. They like grass, but they can also eat meat. When it is cool at night, their bodies cool down. Camels know how to live in tough places.

According to the article, what do camels eat?

▶ What words are important in the question above? *camels* and *eat*

▶ Scan the passage for the key words *camels* and *eat*. To scan is to run your eyes over the passage. You do not need to read every word. Just look for key words.

▶ Read the sentences that have key words carefully. Ask yourself, "Does this sentence answer my question?"

▶ Here is a sentence with the key words *camels* and *eat*: "Still, camels eat and drink their fill." Does it answer the question? No, it does not. Keep looking.

ANSWER: Camels eat everything from grass to meat.

Try It!

Reread the article to answer this question.

According to the passage, how do camels keep cool in the desert?

_____

_____

Read the article. Use the Think About it to guide your reading. Then answer the question. Use the Hint to help you.

Think About It

Read the title. Then ask yourself what most of the sentences will tell about.

Hint

Try to find each fact in the passage. If you cannot find the fact, then you know that answer choice is incorrect.

The Great Lakes

The Great Lakes are six large lakes in the United States. They are called "great" because they are so large. In fact, they are the largest supply of fresh water in the world. Because they are filled with fresh water, these lakes don't have much salt. (Ocean water has a lot of salt.) The Great Lakes are Lake Huron, Lake Ontario, Lake Michigan, Lake Erie, and Lake Superior. The first letters of each spell out the word "HOMES."

Which of these facts about the Great Lakes is included in the passage?

A   the name of each of the Great Lakes

B   the size of the largest Great Lake

C   the names of the states around the Great Lakes

D   the date each Great Lake got its name

CORRECT ANSWER   The first answer choice is correct.

SUPPORTING DETAILS   This fact is given in the passage's sixth sentence. The Great Lakes are Huron, Ontario, Michigan, Erie, and Superior.

INCORRECT ANSWERS   The second answer choice is not correct. The author names the lakes but does not say how big the individual lakes are.

The third answer choice is not correct because the author does not tell which states surround the Great Lakes.

The fourth answer choice is not correct because the author does not tell when the Great Lakes got their names.

Think About It

Read the title. What part of Abraham Lincoln's life will the article tell about?

What is each paragraph mostly about? What details help tell more about these ideas?

What facts are you learning about Abe Lincoln's life? What do these facts tell you about him?

Read the article. Use each Think About It to guide your reading.

Young Abe Lincoln

1   Abraham Lincoln was the sixteenth president of the United States. His childhood was different from that of other important leaders at the time. Most of the presidents before him came from rich families. Lincoln did not. His family had no money and no education. That did not stop him from doing great things.

2   Young Abe was born on February 12, 1809, on a small farm in Kentucky. (The farm was called Sinking Spring.) He was the first president born west of the Appalachian Mountains. Very few people had built homes in that area. It was a tough place to live. Lincoln was born in a one-room log cabin. When he was seven years old, his family was forced to move. They did not have enough money to stay in Kentucky, so they went first to Indiana and then to Illinois.

3   Lincoln's parents, Thomas and Nancy, could not read or write. Abe only went to school for a total of eighteen months, but he did learn to read and write. "I could read, write, and cipher, but that was all," he said years later. (*Cipher* is another word for doing math.) He was taller than most kids, and he was a good wrestler. He liked to chop trees with an ax, but he didn't like to hunt or fish. He didn't want to hurt the animals.

4   Most of all, Abe loved to read. This is how he learned about the world. This is how he became educated. He read every book he could find, no matter what it was about. Reading helped him as president. Although he grew up poor and had very little schooling, most people call Abraham Lincoln one of America's greatest presidents.

Hints

Look for key words in the question and in the answer choices. Find what the passage says about these key words.

Use the Hints to answer the questions below. Circle the letter for each correct answer. Provide supporting details.

1   According to the passage, what did Abe Lincoln love best of all when he was growing up?

   A   to go fishing

   B   to chop trees

   C   to read books

   D   to write stories

Supporting Details: _____

_____

What does the passage say about each answer choice? Looking back at the article will help you find the correct answer.

2   According to the article, which statement is true about Abe Lincoln?

   A   He wrestled well.

   B   He grew up rich.

   C   He lived in Ohio.

   D   He was very short.

Supporting Details: _____

_____

What is the key word in the question? Look for what the passage says about hunting.

3   According to the article, why didn't Abe Lincoln like to hunt?

   A   He didn't like to eat what he caught.

   B   He didn't like being outdoors.

   C   He didn't think he was good at it.

   D   He didn't like the idea of harming animals.

Supporting Details: _____

_____

PAIR SHARE

With your partner, share and discuss your answers and supporting details.

*D*irections
Read this article. Then answer questions 1 through 5.

Scraping the Sky: The Empire State Building

by Gould Martin

The Empire State Building

There is a famous scene in the movie *King Kong*. A giant ape holds a beautiful woman in his hands. He takes her to the top of the Empire State Building. Why does he climb that building and not another? Maybe he climbs it because it is one of the tallest and most well-known structures in the world.

You can find the Empire State Building on the corner of 5th Avenue and West 34th Street in New York City. It is the tallest skyscraper in New York and the third tallest in the United States. (Have you ever wondered where the word *skyscraper* comes from? These buildings are so tall that they almost scrape the sky!)

How tall is tall? Your school might have one, two, or maybe even three floors. The Empire State Building has 103. Do you like to run up and down the stairs in your school sometimes? To reach the 103rd floor of the Empire State Building, you would need to run up 1,860 stair steps.

If that is too much work, or if you're in a hurry, then the Empire State Building has 73 elevators. It also has 6,500 windows. Many of these windows show great views of New York City. The best view, though, is on the 86th floor. That is where you can step out onto the Observation Deck. This is a special area of the building. From there, you can see the city in all directions around you.

Workers began to build the Empire State Building on March 17, 1930. That is St. Patrick's Day, which is an important holiday to some Irish people. In fact, many Irish helped to build the skyscraper, along with others new to the United States. There were Native American workers, too. These workers built the Empire State Building quickly. They raised four floors every week until it was finished in 1931. The building's name comes from New York's nickname: the Empire State.

Not everyone loved the Empire State Building at first. It was not near bus or train lines, so people had trouble getting to it. Also, in 1931 Americans were going through the Great Depression. Many people were out of work. Businesses were not doing well and did not want to pay a lot of money to have offices inside the Empire State Building.

Then, in 1933, *King Kong* came out. In this movie, a giant ape lives on a small island. He is caught and brought to New York City, where he falls in love with a woman named Ann. The ape escapes, grabs Ann, and climbs to the top of the Empire State Building. The scene with Kong and Ann became famous. It also helped to make the Empire State Building one of the most loved buildings in the world.

1 According to information in the article, which sentence about the Empire State Building is **true**?

A The building was not popular with some people at first.

B The building is the world's tallest skyscraper.

C The building was finished in 1933.

D The building has no elevators.

2 Why does the giant ape in *King Kong* climb the Empire State Building and not some other building?

A because it is lit up

B because it is pretty

C because it is well-known

D because Ann likes it

3 Which of these facts about the Empire State Building is included in this passage?

A the number of bathrooms

B the name of its owners

C the time it takes to go to the top

D the year building work began

4 According to the article, what was wrong with where the Empire State Building was built?

A It was not in New York City.

B It was not near bus or train lines.

C It was too close to the water.

D It was near too many businesses.

5 According to the article, the Empire State Building is so tall it almost scrapes the sky. Give **two** details from the article that show how tall it is.

1. _____

_____

_____

2. _____

_____

_____

Answer Form

1 Ⓐ Ⓑ Ⓒ Ⓓ

2 Ⓐ Ⓑ Ⓒ Ⓓ

3 Ⓐ Ⓑ Ⓒ Ⓓ

4 Ⓐ Ⓑ Ⓒ Ⓓ

Number Correct

/4

GPI/CPI

3.R.GPI.1c: Read and understand written directions

Introduction

In this lesson, you will learn about directions. **Directions** tell you how to do something.

Have you ever needed to tell a friend how to play a game? If so, then you gave your friend directions.

Directions are made up of **steps**. Each step gives a different part of the directions. For example, pretend you are learning how to make a paper airplane. One step of the directions might tell you to fold the paper in half. Another step might tell you to get out a sheet of paper.

Wait a minute! Shouldn't you get out a sheet of paper first? Steps must come in the right order. **Sequence** is the order of steps. Sequence tells you which step to do first, which to do next, and so on.

When you read directions, check to see that the sequence of steps makes sense. Also, make sure that no steps are missing. Without all the steps, you can't follow the directions. You might have a paper airplane that doesn't fly!

| directions | = | steps | + | sequence |

Read these directions. Then answer the question below.

Toasted

Making toast is easy, and the food goes well with cereal or by itself. Here is what you need: bread, a toaster, and a topping (such as butter, honey, or jelly).

Step 1: Put two pieces of bread in the toaster. Pull the toaster handle down.

Step 2: When the toast pops up, wait a few minutes for it to cool.

Step 3: Put the slices of toast on a plate.

Step 4: Spread a topping on the toast.

In which step of the directions do you put the toast on a plate?

▶ What do the directions tell how to do? They tell how to make toast.

▶ Each step tells something new about how to make toast. Make sure that all the steps make sense. Look to see that they are in the right order.

▶ Reread each step. Look for which step tells about putting toast on a plate.

▶ Does Step 4 tell you to put the toast on a plate? No, it doesn't. It tells you to spread a topping on the toast.

ANSWER: Step 3 tells you to put toast on a plate.

Try It!

Reread the directions to answer this question.

According to the passage, what are three toppings you might use on toast?

_____

Read the passage. Use the Think About it to guide your reading. Then answer the question. Use the Hint to help you.

Think About It

Read the title carefully. What do you think the directions will tell you to do?

How to Make a Bug Sandwich

Step 1: Put a piece of bologna on a slice of bread. Use bologna because it's round. This is the bug's body.

Step 2: Have an adult cut several black olives in half. Place these on your bologna. These are your bug's spots.

Step 3: Use a round pickle slice for the head.

Step 4: Use two raisins for the eyes.

Step 5: Use four straight pretzels for the legs.

Hint

Following steps is important. But it's also important to know why you're doing each step. What does the bologna need to look like?

In Step 1 of the recipe, why do you use bologna instead of another lunch meat?

A   because it tastes good

B   because it is pink

C   because it is round

D   because it is cold

CORRECT ANSWER   The third answer choice is correct.

SUPPORTING DETAILS   The bologna is round. It should be round because it's the bug's body.

INCORRECT ANSWERS   The first answer choice is not correct. Some people might think bologna tastes good, but that is not why you need it to make a bug sandwich.

The second answer choice is not correct because the passage does not talk about color. It only says the meat should be round.

The fourth answer choice is not correct because the passage does not talk about hot or cold. It only says the meat should be round.

Read the article. Use each Think About It to guide your reading.

Worm Farm

Think About It	

1 To have a great garden, you need fertilizer. Fertilizer helps the soil grow fat, red tomatoes and brightly colored flowers.

2 But where can you get fertilizer? From worms, of course! Here's how to start a worm farm.

What words help you keep track of when to do each step?

3 First, find a large cardboard box. Next, line the inside with a garbage bag to keep the box dry. Now fill your box with soil, worms, and scraps of food. Soil is a special kind of dirt for growing things. You can get the best soil at a garden store. You can also use black dirt from outside.

What can you find at a garden store? What can you use from outside?

4 Worms from your backyard will not work. Instead, use red worms or tiger worms. They will eat the food in your farm and digest it so that it turns into fertilizer. You can find red worms and tiger worms at a garden store.

5 Use scraps of food from your kitchen. Vegetables work best. Don't use citrus fruits, like oranges, because worms hate their smell. The food needs to be in tiny pieces because worms don't have teeth. Put the worms near the bottom of your box and the food on top. The worms will smell the food and wriggle up. But don't give them too much food. If they don't eat it, the food will rot and begin to stink.

Why should you use only a little food? Why should you use only a little water?

6 Spray your soil with a little water. Don't use too much water, though, or your worms will drown.

7 Now, put a cover on your box to keep it dark. Worms like that.

8 After a few weeks, you should have enough fertilizer to help make your garden grow right. Enjoy your tomatoes and flowers!

Hints

Look for words like *first* and *next*. They help you know when to do things.

What do the worms do to turn the soil into fertilizer?

Reread paragraph 6. What does it say about water?

PAIR SHARE

With your partner, share and discuss your answers and supporting details.

Use the Hints to answer the questions below. Circle the letter for each correct answer. Provide supporting details.

1   In the directions, what should you do right after you find a large cardboard box?

  A   Fill the box with soil.

  B   Line the box with a bag.

  C   Add food to the box.

  D   Cover the box with a lid.

  Supporting Details: _____

  _____

2   According to the article, why should you use red worms or tiger worms?

  A   They love to eat citrus fruits.

  B   They have teeth for eating food.

  C   They are found in backyards.

  D   They will eat and digest the food.

  Supporting Details: _____

  _____

3   According to the article, why is it important not to use too much water?

  A   The worms must stay dry.

  B   The worms must not drown.

  C   The worms do not like the smell.

  D   The worms do not like to drink.

  Supporting Details: _____

  _____

Directions
Read this article. Then answer questions 1 through 5.

The Colors of Leaves

by Kelly Jones

Every fall, many trees become rainbows of color. Families pile into their cars to see the wonderful sights of the leaves changing from green to red, yellow, or brown. But did you know that those different colors are inside the leaves all year long? Here is how you can find them.

Before you begin, you will need a few things. Find two to three big leaves. It's okay to use leaves from different trees. You'll also need a scissors or plastic knife, as well as several small glass jars. You'll need rubbing alcohol, a couple of coffee filters, foil, and a bit of tape. You'll also need at least one adult. That person will help you with two of the steps.

First, tear the leaves into tiny pieces. You can use a scissors or a knife to chop and cut up the leaves. Remember to get an adult's help any time you are using something sharp.

Now, put the bits of leaves into several small glass jars. Pour rubbing alcohol into the jars. Pour just enough to cover the leaves. (Don't use the rubbing alcohol without an adult's help. It is dangerous if it is swallowed or gets in your eyes.) Use a plastic knife to cut the leaves more when they are in the alcohol.

Cover the jars with foil, and place them in a tray with hot tap water in it. The water should be hot, but don't make it too hot. You don't want to burn yourself.

Let the jars sit for an hour. If the hot water cools off, empty it out and pour more hot water. Turn the jars every few minutes. You should notice that the liquid is beginning to turn a dark color. These are the colors of your leaves. But wait! The colors are still mixed together.

To un-mix them, find your coffee filters. Filters are a special kind of paper used to make coffee. With your scissors, cut a few filters into long strips. Dip one end of each strip into a jar with your liquid leaves. Bend the other end of the strip out of the jar. Tape its end to the side of the glass jar. Wait two hours.

During that time, you can watch as the liquid slowly disappears. Part of it is evaporating. To evaporate means to turn from liquid to vapor. (Although liquid must stay on the earth's surface, vapor is in the air.) Not all of the liquid evaporates, though. Some of it travels up the coffee filter.

These, finally, are your leaves' different colors. You will see green. You may even see different shades of green. But you should also see other colors as well. Try to tell whether your different leaves have different colors.

The next time you see the leaves change in the fall, remember what you have learned. They were those colors all along!

1 What is the purpose of having adults help in this experiment?

   A They help collect leaves from trees.
   B They help with the rubbing alcohol.
   C They help find coffee filters.
   D They help keep the water hot.

2 Which item do you need for the first step?

   A foil
   B filters
   C leaves
   D jars

3 What do you do **right after** you tear the leaves and put the bits into glass jars?

   A Pour hot tap water into a tray.
   B Turn the jars every few minutes.
   C Cut coffee filters into strips.
   D Pour rubbing alcohol into the jars.

4 If the hot water cools off, then

   A heat the jars in the oven
   B dump it out and pour more in
   C wait another hour or so
   D mix the leaves with alcohol again

5 The chart below shows steps from the experiment.

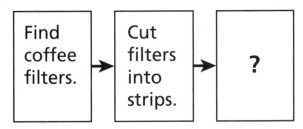

Which step **best** belongs in the empty box?

   A Dip one end into the jar.
   B Bend one end out of the jar.
   C Wait for two hours.
   D Tape one end to the side of the jar.

Answer Form

1 Ⓐ Ⓑ Ⓒ Ⓓ
2 Ⓐ Ⓑ Ⓒ Ⓓ
3 Ⓐ Ⓑ Ⓒ Ⓓ
4 Ⓐ Ⓑ Ⓒ Ⓓ
5 Ⓐ Ⓑ Ⓒ Ⓓ

Number Correct

/ 5

Introduction

In this lesson, you will learn about setting and plot. **Setting** is where and when a story takes place. **Plot** is what happens in the story.

Think about the story's setting. A story about a trip to Mars, for example, needs to be set in outer space and on the planet. The story should also be set in the future. That's because no one has yet been to Mars.

In almost any story, the setting is important. A story set in outer space will have characters who know how to fly spaceships. Those characters will do things that are different than if they had stayed on Earth.

Think about your own life. It has a setting. It is the place where you live and do things. It is also the time you live in. How would your life be different if you lived in another state? In another country? A thousand years ago?

All stories have a plot, too. The plot is made up of events. Events are the things that happen in a story. The **sequence of events** is the order in which events happen. First one event happens, then the next, and so on.

The plot also tells what problems the characters have and the lessons these characters learn. In a story about a trip to Mars, the characters might learn that traveling in space is not easy.

Where and when does the story take place?	What big thing happens?	What problem do the characters try to solve?
in outer space on the planet Mars, in the future	People travel to Mars.	They want to find a way to build a city on Mars.

Read this story. Then answer the question below.

Backyard Visitors

1   Last Saturday, Molly was reading quietly on the couch. Suddenly, her sister Bridget appeared, her eyes wide. "What's going on?" Molly asked.

2   But Bridget didn't say anything. She just put her finger to her lips. She wanted her sister to be quiet.

3   Molly followed Bridget to the backyard. Bridget pointed at something behind the fence. At first, Molly couldn't see anything. But then she did: a mother deer and her fawn. "Oh!" Molly cried. And that's when they ran away.

What happens after Molly cries out?

▶ What main things happen in the story? First, Bridget comes to get Molly. Then, the two sisters creep to the backyard to see something.

▶ Why does Bridget put her finger to her lips? She wants her sister to be quiet.

▶ Why does Bridget want her sister to be quiet? There are a mother deer and her fawn in the backyard. Based on these clues, you can guess that if Molly yells, the deer will run away.

ANSWER: After Molly cries "Oh!" the deer and her fawn run away.

Try It!

Reread the story to answer this question.

What is the setting of "Backyard Visitors"?

_____

_____

Read the poem. Use the Think About it to guide your reading. Then answer the question. Use the Hint to help you.

Think About It

When does the poem take place? How does this setting change?

Hint

First, find where the sun goes down. What is the very next thing that happens?

A Daisy Wants to Grow

A daisy wants to grow.
When the morning sun yawns, so does she,
Stretching way up toward the sky.
When the sun says good night, so does she,
5   Closing her leaves to rest, dreaming of being tall,
Because more than anything,
A daisy wants to grow.

When the sun goes down at night, what does the daisy do first?

A   She dreams of being tall.

B   She says good night.

C   She stretches toward the sky.

D   She yawns and wakes up.

CORRECT ANSWER The second answer choice is correct.

SUPPORTING DETAILS In the fourth line, the sun says good night. The poem then says, "so does she." This means that the daisy also says good night.

INCORRECT ANSWERS The first answer choice is not correct because the daisy only dreams of being tall after saying good night and closing up her leaves.

The third answer choice is not correct because the daisy stretches upward during the day, not at night.

The fourth answer choice is not correct because the daisy wakes up in the morning, not at night.

Think About It

Why do you think the title is "Knight for a Day"? Does the title give a clue about what happens in the story?

Why does Matthew think that life was better in the days of King Arthur?

Why does Matthew fix his hair and stand up straight?

How does Matthew feel at the end of the story?

Read the story. Use each Think About It to guide your reading.

Knight for a Day

1   Matthew was tired and bored. He liked the museum, but his class had been walking around for an hour. He needed a break.

2   That's when he saw it. Up ahead was a shiny suit of armor.

3   Matthew had read about King Arthur and the Knights of the Round Table. They wore armor to protect themselves. They rode horses and rescued beautiful ladies from trouble. *Life was better back then*, Matthew thought to himself. *I want to be a knight.*

4   He looked around him. Mrs. Hedlund was pointing to something in a glass case. Matthew's friends were listening. No one was paying any attention to him, so he slipped away.

5   The armor was so polished and shiny Matthew could see himself in its reflection. He fixed his hair so that it didn't look so messy. He stood up as straight as he could. He turned and looked back at his class. Still, no one was looking at him, so he carefully and quietly climbed into the armor.

6   Inside it was dark and cramped. The armor was heavy, making it hard to move. He could barely see in front of him.

7   Matthew imagined another knight riding directly toward him. The knight's horse snorted, and Matthew couldn't get out of the way. He pulled his horse's reins, but the animal wouldn't move. He didn't know what to do. Being a knight was kind of scary!

8   As carefully as he had climbed in, Matthew climbed out of the armor. His heart was beating fast when he snuck back down the hall. Mrs. Hedlund was still talking. *I'm happy just being a kid*, Matthew thought.

Hints

What details does the author tell about Matthew's day at the museum?

Use the Hints to answer the questions below. Circle the letter for or write out each correct answer. Provide supporting details.

1 Why is Matthew tired and bored? What does he decide to do? Use details from the story in your answer.

Why Matthew is tired and bored: _____

_____

_____

_____

What he decides to do: _____

_____

_____

_____

At the end of the story, what does Matthew think to himself?

2 What is the main thing that Matthew learns in this story?

A   Being a kid is fine.

B   Being a knight is fun.

C   Riding a horse is easy.

D   Wearing armor is simple.

Supporting Details: _____

_____

Hints

What does Matthew imagine while he is inside the armor?

3 Matthew comes to think that being a knight is scary. Give two details from the story that show that being a knight is scary.

1. _____

_____

_____

2. _____

_____

_____

When does Matthew first look at the class? When does he look back?

4 What happens each time Matthew looks at the class?

A The class watches to see what Matthew will do.

B The class keeps paying attention to something else.

C The class keeps walking to different parts of the museum.

D The class looks around, trying to find Matthew.

Supporting Details: _____

_____

PAIR SHARE

With your partner, share and discuss your answers and supporting details.

Directions
Read this story. Then answer questions 1 through 6.

Stop Time

by Nicholson Freeman

Leon pulled Frank aside. He tried to whisper something to him, but the sounds of recess were too loud. Kids were playing kickball and tag. Across the playground, two girls giggled. One of them wore a polka-dot dress.

"What did you say? I can't hear you!" Frank yelled.

"I have a special power!" Leon yelled back, but Frank still could not hear him. So Leon grabbed Frank's hand and then snapped his fingers three times.

Everything went silent. There was no noise from kickball or tag. Across the playground, no girls giggled.

Frank looked around, but he could not believe what he saw. The kids playing kickball and tag were still there. So were the girls. But they had all stopped, as if frozen. One kid who had been running was in mid-stride. He was partly in the air. Leon pointed at the girl in the polka-dot dress. Her mouth was open. She had been in the middle of saying something.

"What happened?" Frank whispered.

"I stopped time," Leon said.

"You did what?" Frank said, and this time he didn't whisper. Nobody moved. Not one of the kids had heard him.

Leon began walking toward the red rubber ball the kids had been using to play kickball. As he walked, he told Frank that he had known about his special power for two days. On Saturday, he was snapping his fingers along to music, and suddenly everything stopped. It took him a while to figure out how to start time back up again.

"It felt like forever!" Leon said. But of course it didn't matter how long it took. When time started again, no one knew that time had ever stopped at all. The clock didn't miss a tick.

Leon reached the ball and gave it a great kick. "I'm getting better at it, though," he said. "I was even able to stop time for everyone else without stopping you!" After stepping back a few paces so he was out of the way, he snapped his fingers three times. The noise of recess flooded back into Frank's ears. He heard a kid shout, "Hey! Where's our ball?"

Leon then told Frank about his big plan. No one else knew about his special power, and he was finally going to put it to use. Frank wasn't so sure about Leon's plan, but he kept his mouth shut—mostly.

Later that day, Mrs. Martinez said the class was going to have a spelling test. She read the words from a sheet of paper on her desk.

Leon hated spelling. It was his worst subject. When Mrs. Martinez wasn't looking, he snapped his fingers three times. Just as it always did, time stopped.

Leon walked up to the front of the class. *This test is going to be easy*, he thought. But when he grabbed the sheet of paper to look at the words, his eyes grew wide with surprise. Instead of spelling words, the paper said the following:

> Dear Leon,
>
> How dare you cheat! Now snap your fingers and say you're sorry.

1 Where does the **first** part of the story take place?

   A on a playground

   B in a classroom

   C in Frank's room

   D on a school bus

2 What is the surprise at the end of the story?

   A Frank likes the girl in the polka-dot dress.

   B Leon learns how to stop time by snapping his fingers.

   C Mrs. Martinez finds out about Leon's special power.

   D Leon kicks the red rubber ball when time is stopped.

3 What is Leon's **main** problem in the story?

   A He doesn't know how to stop his special power.

   B He wants to get out of taking a spelling test.

   C Frank does not believe that he has a special power.

   D The other schoolchildren think he is strange.

4 How does Mrs. Martinez **most likely** find out about Leon's special power?

   A She also has a special power.

   B She reads about it in the newspaper.

   C The girls tell her about the power.

   D Frank tells her about the power.

5 According to the story, when does Leon **first** learn about his special power?

   A during recess with Frank

   B while listening to music

   C while taking a test

   D before playing ball

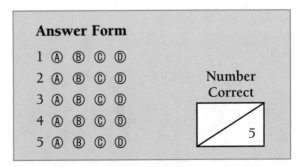

Answer Form

1 Ⓐ Ⓑ Ⓒ Ⓓ

2 Ⓐ Ⓑ Ⓒ Ⓓ

3 Ⓐ Ⓑ Ⓒ Ⓓ

4 Ⓐ Ⓑ Ⓒ Ⓓ

5 Ⓐ Ⓑ Ⓒ Ⓓ

Number Correct

/5

6 What is Leon's special power? What happens the first time Leon uses his power? Use details from the story in your answer.

Leon's special power: _____

_____

What happens the first time Leon uses his power: _____

_____

GPI/CPI

3.R.GPI.2k: Describe characters, their actions, and their motivations

3.R.GPI.2l: Use knowledge of story structure, story elements, and key vocabulary to interpret stories

Introduction

In this lesson, you will learn about characters. A **character** is who a story is about. Characters can be people or animals. They can be realistic or like people in the real world. They can also be make-believe.

Stories tell what characters do and how they solve problems. In that way, characters are important to the plot, or the things that happen. After all, without characters, nothing big would happen in the first place!

Characters are like real people in other ways, too. They don't just do things. They do things for reasons. Why a character does something is called that character's **motivation**. You do things for reasons, too. Maybe you play sports because you like being outside. Maybe you put your umbrella in the front closet so that you won't lose it.

Finally, you can learn about one character by comparing it to another. Are the two characters alike? Do they love the same things? Do they do things for the same reasons? Or are they very different from each other?

Ask yourself these questions to help you understand characters.

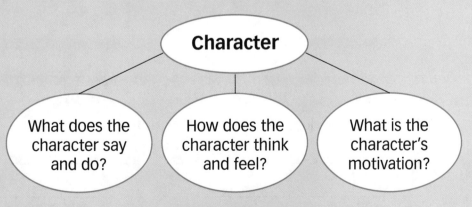

Character

- What does the character say and do?
- How does the character think and feel?
- What is the character's motivation?

Read this story. Then answer the question below.

When Dad Was a Boy

1   One day Dad told me about a job he had when he was a kid. He wanted a new bike, but his parents did not have much money. Grandpa told him he could make money delivering newspapers to people's houses. Dad did not like the idea, but he really wanted that bike.

2   He got the job and planned to quit when he got the bike. He worked all summer, and he paid for his bike. After that, Dad changed his mind about working. He decided to keep his job, and he used his new bike to help.

How does Dad most likely feel when he decides to keep his job?

▶ At the beginning of the story, what does Dad think? He does not want to get a job. He wants his parents to get him a bike, but they don't have the money.

▶ What does Dad do? He gets a job anyway so he can buy the bike. He sets a goal for himself.

▶ Does Dad meet his goal of getting a bike? Yes. He even decides to keep his job.

▶ How do people usually feel when they meet their goals? They feel proud.

ANSWER: Dad most likely feels proud.

Try It!

Reread the story to answer this question.

What word best describes Dad in the story?

_____

_____

Read the story. Use the Think About It to guide your reading. Then answer the question. Use the Hint to help you.

Maria and Maria Luna

1   Papi was upset with me. I hadn't been helping out at home as he and Mom had asked. "Maria," he said. "Let me tell you about your grandmother."

2   He told me how hard Maria Luna worked. Her tortillas were so good that her company got bigger. At that time, few Latinas were bosses. Hearing about her made me think. I was named after her. I wanted to work hard like her, too.

Why does Papi tell Maria the story of Maria Luna?

A   He wants Maria to learn to work harder.

B   He wants Maria to know how she got her name.

C   He wants Maria to learn how to make tortillas.

D   He wants Maria to visit her grandmother.

Think About It

What does Maria think after Papi tells her the story of Maria Luna?

Hint

You can use what you know about people to figure out why characters do what they do.

CORRECT ANSWER The first answer choice is correct.

SUPPORTING DETAILS In the first paragraph, the author says that Maria has not been helping out. After Papi tells the story of Maria Luna, Maria wants to work hard.

INCORRECT ANSWERS The second answer choice is not correct because the author does not explain why Maria was named after Maria Luna.

The third answer choice is not correct because Maria does not talk about making her own tortillas.

The fourth answer choice is not correct because Papi wants Maria to learn something from Maria Luna's story. He does not ask Maria to visit anyone.

Read the passage. Use each Think About It to guide your reading.

The House on Packer Street

Think About It

What kind of place is the house on Packer Street?

How does Li feel about walking home in the cold rain?

How does Li react to what happens? How would people you know react if these things were happening to them?

1   Everyone said that the big old house on Packer Street was haunted. Brad said it was filled with spooky ghosts. Candice thought that pirates went there to count their gold. And Yasmin swore that she'd once seen a witch in the upstairs window.

2   But Li knew the real story. She'd found out one cold, rainy day last October.

3   Li was walking down the street after school, trying to keep her umbrella from blowing away in the wind. She sang a happy little song to herself when, all of the sudden, a black cat sprang in front of her. "Rooowrrr!" the cat growled. Then it sprang away once more, up the steps to the old Packer Street house.

4   Well, Li decided to follow that cat up to the front door of the house. "Why kitty, let me help. You're simply soaked!" she said.

5   She knocked on the door and waited and waited. Finally, after what seemed like an hour, the door creaked open . . .

6   And there stood an actual, real-life pirate! He had it all: a peg leg, an eye patch, and a parrot on his shoulder. Behind him, a shadowy, see-through person asked, "Who is it, Gary? Don't let them just stand out there and get soaked! Invite them in."

7   Li smiled. So it was all true after all. The house really did have a pirate and a ghost in it. Li could also see a witch peeking out from behind an old staircase.

8   In the end, though, the house was quite a nice place. Li fed the black cat some treats, she had some hot cocoa, and she learned that Hide and Seek is hard to play with a ghost!

Use the Hints to answer the questions below. Circle or write out each correct answer. Provide supporting details.

Think about how Li acts when walking in the rain. What does she do when she finds out who lives in the house?

1   Which word best describes Li in the story?

  A   unbelieving

  B   talkative

  C   scared

  D   brave

  Supporting Details: _____

  _____

Why does Li walk up to the house in the first place? What is her reason for knocking on the door?

2   In the story, Li most likely wishes to

  A   make sure the cat is safe.

  B   find out who lives in the house.

  C   find a dry place out of the rain.

  D   get away from the growling cat.

  Supporting Details: _____

  _____

Reread the parts of the story that tell about the ghost. These parts give clues to what kind of character the ghost is.

3   The ghost is friendly in the story. Give two details from the story that show the ghost is friendly.

  1. _____

  _____

  _____

  2. _____

  _____

  _____

Hints

Reread the first paragraph. What do Brad, Candice, and Yasmin say about the house on Packer Street?

Reread paragraph 3 and paragraph 7. These paragraphs give important details about why Li does what she does in the story.

4 Which sentence best describes the other children in this story?

A The children enjoy spending time outside the house on Packer Street.

B The children enjoy thinking about what goes on at the house on Packer Street.

C The children enjoy daring Li to walk up to the house on Packer Street.

D The children enjoy visiting those who live in the house on Packer Street.

5 How does Li feel about what she finds at the house on Packer Street? What does she do to show how she feels? Use details from the story in your answer.

How Li feels about what she sees: _____

_____

_____

What Li does to show her feelings: _____

_____

_____

PAIR SHARE

With your partner, share and discuss your answers and supporting details.

Directions
Read the passage. Then answer questions 1 through 6.

Wilkommen to Germany!

by Kai Sanders

The whole plane ride from New York to Frankfurt, Germany, James was full of questions.

"Do they have pizza in Germany?" he asked as he picked at his airplane meal. It was a soggy turkey sandwich.

"Who cares?" James's older brother, Ryan, asked. "It's not like it will taste the same as our pizza anyway."

Their mother rolled her eyes and said, "Yes, James, there will be pizza. But there will also be other new foods you might want to try." James nodded. He *was* ready to try all kinds of German foods.

James and Ryan were going to Germany because their mom had an important work meeting there. During the day, they would visit their aunt, who had lived in Germany for five years. At night, they would see the sights with Mom. And on the weekend, they would drive around and see things like old Roman farm ruins and villages that had been around for more than 600 years!

As the plane flew across the Atlantic, James found it harder to sit still. Why weren't they in Germany yet? He checked his map and tried to guess where they were over the ocean. He watched a movie. Time was moving too slowly.

Mom calmly read her magazine, but Ryan just seemed to get grouchier and grouchier. He put on some headphones and sank back into his seat. "Just tell me when we're there," he said.

After a few more hours, Mom nudged James. He'd somehow drifted off to sleep. "Good news," she said. "We're landing now. We're in Germany!"

As James squirmed and hurried to put his pillow and book into his backpack, Ryan looked like he could sleep for another two days. "Now, James," Mom said, "no need to rush. We'll be there soon."

"We're here! We're here! We're here!" James cried.

"I know. I know. I know," Ryan muttered. "Big deal."

When they got off the plane, James could already see that Germany was different from New York. Most of the signs were in German, for starters. It was a good thing Aunt Gretchen would be there to help them.

As the family left the airport, they found Gretchen waiting for them outside. "*Wilkommen!*" Gretchen said. She grinned and threw her arms open for hugs.

James looked at Ryan. Ryan looked at James. What had she just said?

Mom leaned over and whispered, "Don't worry. *Wilkommen* just means 'welcome' in German."

James smiled. "*Wilkommen* back to you!" he said as he gave his aunt a hug.

"Wilko . . . oh, forget it," Ryan said, clinging to his suitcase. "The words are too long here." James could see then that Ryan didn't just look grouchy. He looked maybe a little scared. His shoulders were hunched the same way they were before he had to take math tests at school.

"Here, I'll help you," James said. "The 'w' is like a 'v.' So it's like you're saying 'vilk,' then 'o,' then 'men.'"

Ryan said the word, softly at first, and then a little more loudly. "Okay," he said. "I guess I just need to get used to things over here."

And James, who loved adventure and trying new things, thought he was beginning to understand why Ryan had been grouchy. He also promised himself that no matter what, he would do his best to make sure Ryan had just as much fun as he planned to have. First up, though, was looking for a place to try some German pizza.

1 In the story, Ryan is **mostly**

   A excited
   B unhappy
   C cheerful
   D saddened

2 How are James and Ryan alike?

   A They are both going to Germany for the first time.
   B They are both happy about their trip to Germany.
   C They both think some German words are too long.
   D They both feel nervous about going to Germany.

3 Read these sentences from the story.

   "Wilkommen!" **Gretchen said. She grinned and threw her arms open for hugs.**

   These sentences show that Gretchen

   A knows that the boys want an adventure
   B misses living in New York
   C is happy about visiting Germany
   D is happy to see her nephews

Answer Form

1 Ⓐ Ⓑ Ⓒ Ⓓ
2 Ⓐ Ⓑ Ⓒ Ⓓ
3 Ⓐ Ⓑ Ⓒ Ⓓ

4 When the plane lands in Frankfurt, James is

A uncaring
B afraid
C thankful
D grouchy

5 Give two examples from the story that show Mom is patient.

1. _____

_____

2. _____

_____

6 James becomes more and more eager in the story. Give **two** examples from the story that show James is eager.

1. _____

_____

2. _____

_____

Answer Form	Number Correct
4 Ⓐ Ⓑ Ⓒ Ⓓ	4

Punctuation and Capitalization

GPI/CPI

3.W.CPI.3: Use basic punctuation correctly

3.W.CPI.5: Capitalize words such as literary titles, holidays, and product names

Introduction

In this lesson, you will learn how to make sure your writing is clear. This means learning to use correct punctuation and capitalization. **Punctuation** is all the marks we use in words or sentences to help readers know what we mean. Some common punctuation marks are periods (.), question marks (?), and exclamation points (!). Punctuation helps you know where one sentence ends and another begins. It helps in other ways, too.

You use **capital letters** at the beginning of words. Most proper nouns start with capital letters. That shows that those words are special. Names are proper nouns. So are holidays and book titles. You might even have seen the names of products, or things you buy, in capital letters.

To make sure your writing is correct, keep a checklist. A **checklist** is a list of rules. Your checklist might remind you to use question marks correctly. It might remind you to capitalize the first word in a sentence. When you are finished writing, check to make sure that you have followed all the rules on your checklist.

Checklist for Finding Mistakes

Punctuation	Capital Letters
☐ All statements should end with periods.	☐ A capital letter should begin each sentence.
☐ All questions should end with question marks.	☐ The word *I* is always capitalized.
☐ Sentences showing excitement may end in exclamation points.	☐ Proper names should begin with capital letters.

Read the paragraph. Draw a line through each part that has a mistake, and write the correction above the mistake. Then read the corrected paragraph.

Last night my family ate Pizza for dinner. My sister suzie wouldn't eat it, though? She only likes tacos, ice cream, and green beans.

Last night my family ate ~~Pizza~~ pizza for dinner. My sister ~~suzie~~ Suzie wouldn't eat it, though? She only likes tacos, ice cream, and green beans.

Let's look at how the author corrected the errors in the paragraph.

▶ Reread the first sentence. Are there any mistakes? Yes. The word *pizza* is not a proper noun. It is not special in the sentence. It should not be capitalized.

▶ Reread the second sentence. Are there any mistakes? Yes. The word *suzie* should begin with a capital letter. That is because *Suzie* is a name. It is a proper noun. Also, the sentence should end with a period, not a question mark. The author is not asking a question here.

▶ Reread the third sentence. Are there any mistakes? No. The sentence is correct as it is written.

Try It! Draw a line through each mistake, and write the correction above the line.

Next saturday, do You want to go to the park with me! I'm going with Hanna and pete.

Read the paragraph. Use the Think About It to guide your reading. Draw a line through each part that has a mistake, and write the correction above the mistake.

Think About It

Do any words seem like they should be in capital letters or not in capital letters? What punctuation marks would you change?

Two Furry Surprises

One day, my mom told us she had a surprise. "do you know what I have?" she asked. Then she opened her bag. Out crawled two kittens? My sister's face lit up, and she clapped her hands with joy. "We'll call them itty and Bitty," i said.

As you correct the paragraph, remember to look back at the checklist on page 117. It will help you make sure you remember some rules for using correct punctuation and capital letters.

CORRECT ANSWERS The first sentence is correct as is.

The second sentence should read, "'Do you know what I have?' she asked." The first word of a sentence always begins with a capital letter.

The third sentence is correct as is.

The fourth sentence should read, "Out crawled two kittens!" This sentence is not a question. Instead, it shows excitement. It needs an exclamation point.

The fifth sentence is correct as is.

The last sentence should read, "'We'll call them Itty and Bitty,' I said." Names always begin with capital letters. So does the word *I*.

Think About It

How can you tell when an author is asking a question? How can you tell when an author is making a statement?

Which words should begin with capital letters? Which words should not begin with capital letters?

Read each paragraph and find the mistakes. Draw a line through each mistake in the paragraph. Then write the correction above it. Use each Think About It to guide your reading.

1 My dad pulled out a picture from a box in the living room. It showed him as a little kid. After staring at the picture, i asked, "Is this really you." It both looked like him and didn't look like him. He had more hair then? also, he wears glasses now.

2 Dad told me about the Neighborhood where he grew up. It was downtown. cars, buses, and bikes rushed by at all hours. While he was falling asleep at night, he could hear the buzz of the street. But dad's life is different now. We live near two cornfields?

Think About It

Remember the rules for using capital letters. How should you write out book titles?

Read the paragraph and find the mistakes. Draw a line through each mistake in the paragraph. Then write the correction above it. Use the Think About It to guide your reading.

3   Dear lucy,

Thank you for coming to my party. It was nice to see you, and i had a lot of fun. Thank you, too, for the book. I can't wait to read <u>The Lazy lizard</u>. Have you read it.

Thanks again,

Jason

PAIR SHARE

With your partner, share and discuss your answers and supporting details.

1 Here is a paragraph a student wrote about her favorite sport. The paragraph has some mistakes in capital letters and punctuation. Some sentences may have no mistakes. There are <u>no</u> mistakes in spelling.

Read the paragraph, and find the mistakes. Draw a line through each mistake in the paragraph. Then write the correction above it.

My favorite sport is volleyball. I play it every day after School.

It helps that I am tall. When my friends set the ball, I can spike it

over the net. My brother carlos likes baseball better! it's easier for

him because he is shorter. Do you have a favorite sport.

2 Here is a paragraph a student wrote about visiting her grandmother. The paragraph has some mistakes in capital letters and punctuation. Some sentences may have no mistakes. There are <u>no</u> mistakes in spelling.

Read the paragraph, and find the mistakes. Draw a line through each mistake in the paragraph. Then write the correction above it.

> In August, my sister and i visited my grandma. She lives in albany,
>
> New York. We stayed for a weekend! We played at the park, and we
>
> went on a hike. then we helped her make dinner. At night we played
>
> games. We even drank hot cocoa?

3 Here is a paragraph a student wrote about a class field trip. The paragraph has some mistakes in capital letters and punctuation. Some sentences may have no mistakes. There are <u>no</u> mistakes in spelling.

Read the paragraph, and find the mistakes. Draw a line through each mistake in the paragraph. Then write the correction above it.

> On monday, we visited the rose gardens at the museum. Before we
>
> went, we read the book <u>Roses Are red</u>. We learned that roses come in
>
> different colors? At the garden, we saw yellow, white, and red roses.
>
> All in all, it was a Fun trip.

4 Here is a paragraph a student wrote about a made-up holiday. The paragraph has some mistakes in capital letters and punctuation. Some sentences may have no mistakes. There are <u>no</u> mistakes in spelling.

Read the paragraph, and find the mistakes. Draw a line through each mistake in the paragraph. Then write the correction above it.

I decided to make up my own holiday. It's called snake Day

because I really love snakes. I love rattlesnakes, copperheads, and

even plain old Garden snakes. On my holiday, everyone would have to

learn about snakes. My little brother sean would even have to touch

one? He hates snakes!

GPI/CPI

3.W.GPI.1h: Support interpretations with evidence from text

3.W.GPI.2c: Produce responses to stories read or listened to

3.W.GPI.3c: Support ideas

Introduction

In this lesson, you will learn about responding to texts. To **respond** means to think about a passage and then answer a question about it.

First, make sure you understand the question. Read it twice if you need to. If the question has more than one part, read both parts before beginning to write. Also, make sure you answer both parts.

Then you should reread the text. As you read, think about the question you are being asked. What ideas do you have about the passage? Why do you think that way? For example, read these sentences:

> Ty practiced his violin. He loved to play. He played every day.

If someone asked you to tell about Ty, you might say that Ty is good at playing the violin. That's your idea. You got that idea based on details from the passage.

Use details to support your ideas. To **support** means to back up. You can state those details in your own words, or you can use the writer's words. Use the chart below to help you find details to support your ideas.

What question are you being asked?	What idea do you have about the passage?	What details support this idea?
How would you describe Ty?	Ty is good at playing the violin.	Ty practiced his violin. He loved to play. He played every day.

Read this story. Then answer the question below.

In the Headlights

1   Last night, Dad and Topher were in the car and pulling up the driveway. It wasn't late, but it was dark already. Topher sat in the backseat with the window down. The fall wind blew cold against his face. The stars scowled. As Dad drove up to the house, the dead leaves crunched under his tires. And that's when Topher saw the two eyes and nothing else.

2   Topher felt a chill. "It's a ghost!" he yelled. Dad flipped on his bright lights, and that's when they saw the raccoon. It ran away like a thief in the night.

In the story, why does Topher think he sees a ghost?

▶ In paragraph 1, what does the author tell about? He tells about how dark it is. He also tells about the cold wind and the sound of dead leaves. These details help create a spooky mood. They show that Topher might be scared.

▶ Also in paragraph 1, the author writes that the stars "scowled." Things scowl when they are angry. This supports the idea that Topher might be scared.

▶ The author then writes that Topher sees two eyes that are not connected to anything else.

ANSWER: Topher thinks he sees a ghost because he is scared and then sees two eyes that are not connected to anything else.

Try It!

Reread the story to answer this question.

How does Topher probably feel at the very end of the story? Why?

_____

Read the poem. Use the Think About It to guide your reading. Then answer the question. Use the Hint to help you.

Think About It

Read the title. Then ask yourself what the surprise might be.

Hint

What is the secret? How does the speaker of the poem know?

The Surprise

Mom couldn't keep the surprise a secret

As it grew bigger and bigger,

As it bulged rounder and rounder.

Mom couldn't keep the surprise a secret

5   When Dad climbed up into the attic one day

And came down with my old crib.

Mom couldn't keep the surprise a secret,

So one night she gathered us kids around

And told us what we already knew!

Mom has a secret. Give two details from the poem that help give the secret away.

1. _____

2. _____

BEST RESPONSE   1. Mom is growing bigger and bigger. 2. Dad gets the crib down from the attic.

SUPPORTING DETAILS   Mom has a secret that she is trying to keep. This secret is given away when the speaker sees that she is growing bigger and rounder. Dad also climbs into the attic and comes down with a crib. It is clear that Mom is going to have a baby. The baby is growing inside Mom. That's why Mom is getting bigger. When the baby is born, he or she will sleep in the speaker's old crib.

Read the article. Use each Think About It to guide your reading.

A Man of Many Words

Think About It

What questions will this passage answer?

Why did the students need better books in their classrooms?

Why did Webster call his spellers "American books for American children"?

What does the author mean when he says that Webster "helped unite America"?

1   You probably have used a dictionary. Dictionaries are full of words, but who put them there? And who decided how to spell the words? In the United States, that person was Noah Webster.

2   Webster was born in Connecticut in 1758. He studied law but liked teaching more. Webster liked kids, and he thought students needed better books in their classrooms. Not all of his students used the same kind of English. When they spoke words, they said them aloud in different ways. They spelled them differently. Like Webster's students, the books spelled words differently, too.

3   Webster decided that America needed one set of spellings. He thought that this would help unite its people. He created spelling books and sold them in all thirteen states. He called them "American books for American children." In his spelling books, he changed the spelling of *musick* to *music*. He changed *centre* to *center*. Not every change worked, however. He changed *women* to *wimmen*, but the new spelling didn't catch on. People didn't start spelling it Webster's way.

4   When he was finished with his spellers, Webster worked on his dictionary. He didn't just want kids to spell the same way. He wanted all Americans to agree on spelling. He published his first dictionary in 1806, but even after that he kept on working. There were always more words to collect! He finished in 1828, when he was seventy years old. His dictionary was called the *American Dictionary of the English Language*, and it had 70,000 words.

5   In the end, Noah Webster did more than just collect words. He helped unite America.

Hints

Reread paragraph 2. This paragraph explains why Webster wanted to make books for children.

Look at paragraph 3. It tells about some of the words that Noah Webster changed.

1 According to the article, Noah Webster's students used different kinds of English. What are two ways that they used English differently?

1. _____

_____

_____

2. _____

_____

_____

2 In his spelling books, Noah Webster changed the spellings of some common words. Complete the chart below with Webster's new spellings. One box has been filled in for you.

Old Spelling	New Spelling
musick	music
centre	
women	

PAIR SHARE

With your partner, share and discuss your answers and supporting details.

Directions
Read this story. Then answer questions 1 and 2.

Chasing the Wind

by Hiram Jones

Pedro had taken walks hundreds of times before. He had sniffed the streets of Rochester for squirrels and for rabbits. He had sniffed them for cats and for other dogs. He had tugged at his leash, turning around corners and running up the blocks. And his tongue had hung out the whole way. He loved Rochester, but he had never been here alone. Until today, that is.

How had this happened? As the sun began to set and his stomach grumbled, Pedro tried to remember. His day had begun as it always did, with him jumping into bed with Lucia. The girl rubbed the sleep out of her eyes and fed Pedro his usual scoop of kibble. Pedro ate it as fast as he could, slopped up a few sips of water, and then went to the door, his tail wagging. Then Lucia attached the long red leash to Pedro's collar. She opened the back door, and they were off!

Pedro barked happily. He wanted to go faster. He wanted to chase every smell he sniffed. But Lucia wanted them to walk more slowly, especially in the morning. She wasn't in a hurry. After all, it was Saturday, and she didn't have to catch the bus to school. To Pedro, though, all the days were the same. They were full of squirrels and rabbits and cats and other dogs. And on this day, he caught a whiff of something. What was it?

This smell was new and wonderful. It mixed the meow of a cat with the chirp of a squirrel. It smelled delicious, like a rabbit. It made him happy. All the muscles in his body tightened, and he lifted his head into the smell. Pedro tugged at his leash one last time, and Lucia couldn't hold on. Suddenly, Pedro was free.

He chased the wind for blocks, past old Rochester buildings and new apartments. He chased the wind past sweet-smelling shops and tempting garbage cans. He chased the wind until finally he was out of breath. His tongue fell almost down to the sidewalk. The smell was gone, and Pedro was lost.

He sat down. He had been running all day, and now the smells were strange. A young girl and her dog strolled by. The puppy was tiny compared to Pedro and much better behaved. She looked happy. The young girl stayed far away from Pedro, and she told her dog, "No, girl. Stay with me. Good girl." Pedro felt lonely. He missed Lucia and the kibble and the warm bed in the morning. He missed their walks and tugging on the leash. He decided that the next time he went for a walk with Lucia, he would be a very good dog.

But as the shadows grew longer and the sun dipped lower, Pedro gave up. He lay down and put his head on his paws. He let out a sigh. And that's when he heard it: a familiar voice from far down the block. "Pedro!"

1 What makes Pedro excited during his walk with Lucia? How does this cause him to get lost? Use details from the story in your answer.

What makes Pedro excited: _____

_____

How this causes him to get lost: _____

_____

2 At the end of the story, Pedro feels lonely. Give **two** examples from the story that show Pedro is lonely.

1. _____

_____

2. _____

_____

Introduction

In this lesson, you will learn about listening. You listen every day, of course. You listen to music. You listen to the wind blow. But the listening in this lesson is different.

Listening is more than just hearing. Listening means hearing and understanding. When you listen to an article or a story, it is important to understand what the speaker is saying.

As you listen the first time, try not to let your mind wander. Instead, ask yourself important questions. Why did the author write this passage? What is it mostly about? Listen for important details. Remember that details tell more about the main idea. Also, think about the things you don't know. Are there words you don't understand? Are there parts of the passage that don't seem very clear?

As you listen the second time, write down any questions you have. Write down the main idea and important details. Write down facts or the names of characters. Write down whatever will help you remember the passage. Remember that listening isn't just hearing. It's hard work!

| listening | = | thinking about passage | + | asking questions | + | taking notes |

You are now going to listen to a story called "Going Back." You may take notes below as you listen to the story.

Notes

In the story, why doesn't the speaker in the story need to travel very far?

▶ In the first part of the story, what does the speaker tell about? He tells about his trips in the time machine.

▶ In past trips, where does the speaker go in his time machine? He travels to the first Thanksgiving and to the moon landing.

▶ At the end of the story, the speaker says that today he won't go far back in time. He will only go back to last night. Why is last night important?

ANSWER: The speaker doesn't need to travel very far because he just needs to study for his history test.

Try It!

Now answer this question based on the story.

Why does the speaker need a special suit when he goes to the moon landing?

_____

_____

You are now going to listen to a story called "The Rec Center." You may take notes below as you listen to the story.

Notes

Think About It

Why do the girls need old clothes and shovels? What are they about to do?

Hint

Add up the clues the author gives throughout the story. Which answer seems most likely?

From the story, the reader can tell that the girls

A   will be working in a garden.

B   will be walking a nature trail.

C   will be playing a game of tag.

D   will be throwing a baseball.

CORRECT ANSWER   The first answer choice is correct.

SUPPORTING DETAILS   In the story, the girls are working outside. They need old clothes and a shovel. That probably means they will be working in the garden.

INCORRECT ANSWERS   The second answer choice is not correct because you don't need a shovel to walk a nature trail.

The third answer choice is not correct because it does not involve digging in the dirt.

The fourth answer choice is not correct because throwing a baseball is not the same as working outside.

Think About It

You are going to listen to a story called "This Old House." Then you will answer three questions about the story. You will listen to the story twice. The first time you hear the story, listen carefully but do not take notes. As you listen to the story the second time, you may want to take notes using the Think About It questions as a guide.

Notes

What is the setting of the story? What is the weather like?

Why is Julian restless?

Why does Julian miss his old house?

What happens when Julian goes into the kitchen pantry?

Why is Julian nervous at the end of the story?

Hints

Think about the beginning of the story. How does Julian feel, and what does he do?

What is the story mostly about?

Think about the end of the story. What does Julian want to find out? What does he decide to do?

With your partner, share and discuss your answers and supporting details.

1 Why can't Julian sit still? What does he decide to do because of this? Use details from the story in your answer.

Why Julian can't sit still: _____

_____

_____

What he decides to do: _____

_____

_____

2 Which sentence is most important to the main idea of the story?

A "He missed the house he used to live in even if it was smaller."

B "All he knew for sure about these picture-people was that they were his relatives."

C "He wondered what kind of house they had lived in."

D "The passageway was long, narrow, and dark."

Supporting Details: _____

_____

3 According to the story, Julian will most likely

A learn where the passageway leads.

B quickly turn around and go back.

C decide he would rather have a snack.

D run out into the rain, thunder, and lightning.

Supporting Details: _____

_____

Directions

In this part of the lesson, you are going to listen to a story called "American Gothic."
Then you will answer questions 1 through 6 about the story.

You will listen to the story twice. The first time you hear the story, listen carefully but do
not take notes. As you listen to the story the second time, you may want to take notes.
Use the space below for your notes. You may use these notes to answer the questions that
follow.

Notes

1 What is this story **mostly** about?

   A a girl learning what she thinks about a farm
   B a girl getting over her fear of chickens
   C a girl who learns to love life in the city
   D a girl who shops for shoes and handbags

2 Why did the author **most likely** write "American Gothic"?

   A to give information about a famous painting
   B to entertain readers with an interesting story
   C to tell about what Iowa is like during the summer
   D to give readers ideas for places to visit on vacation

3 Read the chart below.

Things That Surprise Nell
the blazing heat
?
Iowa isn't perfectly flat

Which phrase **best** completes the chart?

   A how little it rained
   B the size of the milk cows
   C the number of cornfields
   D how few trees there were

Answer Form

1 Ⓐ Ⓑ Ⓒ Ⓓ
2 Ⓐ Ⓑ Ⓒ Ⓓ
3 Ⓐ Ⓑ Ⓒ Ⓓ

4 Read this sentence from the story.

> **When she got back to the house, she was tired and filthy.**

In this sentence, the word "filthy" **most likely** means

A clean
B fresh
C dirty
D washed

5 Where does Nell's mom tell her she will spend the summer? What does Nell think about it? Use details from the story in your answer.

Where Nell will spend the summer: _____

_____

What Nell thinks about it: _____

_____

6 At the end of the story, Nell decides she likes life on the farm. Give **two** examples of things she likes to do on the farm.

1. _____

_____

2. _____

_____

Answer Form	Number Correct
4 Ⓐ Ⓑ Ⓒ Ⓓ	/ 4

©Curriculum Associates   Copying is not permitted.